BREAKFAST WITH JESUS...

A Holy Invitation with Many Graces

1

Sister Ave Clark, O.P.
Heart to Heart Ministry
718-428-2471
Pearlbud7@aol.com
www.h2h.nyc

Rachel Prayer Hour: post abortion syndrome
Elizabeth Ministry: for parents who lost a child
Caring Hearts: for people with PTSD
Samaritan Hearts: for victims of tragic crimes
SOS: for survivors of suicide
Roses: for survivors of abuse/violence/domestic
       violence
ACOA: for Adult Children of Alcoholics
Caritas: for family with children and adults
       with a disability
Hearts Afire: domestic violence sessions (individually)
Lights in the Darkness: for persons seeking
                 healing from depression
Bereavement Sessions: From the Heart (individual)
Spiritual Direction: Open your Heart (individual)
Pastoral Prayerline: A Listening Heart
Podcast Nun ... Everyday Graces
Podcast Nun 2 ... Heart Conversations
Heart to Heart Prayer Chats: Across the Country

Only the wings of Love and Compassion
can lift and carry us ...

BREAKFAST WITH JESUS . . .

A Holy Invitation with Many Graces

Sister Ave Clark, O.P.
Joseph M. Clark

FRONT COVER
Breakfast with Jesus
Completed painting September 2, 2021

By Susan Pussilano

Catize@optonline.net

What a privilege for me to be a part of the collaboration of such a lovely, timeless and profound meditation on Breakfast with Our Lord.

This piece depicts the early morning sunrise with bursts of inexplainable hues of brilliancy shining on the sea as an introduction to the hope of a new day. The shimmering water is mesmerizing and somehow reminds us of the peace that lies within… the peace that surpasses all human understanding. The gentle lapping waves along with the tender morning breeze serenades and brings comfort.

An old and much revered fishing boat rests after a fine catch and rocks gently to and fro with the rhythm of the sea as creaking sounds escape its tired hull. The fishermen gather around Jesus who serves and feeds them with unbridled humility as only he can. Their speech is soft spoken and grateful as they continue to contemplate this Jesus and the breaking of bread. This is Holy Ground as it encompasses God's magnificent creation along with the importance and significance of being present every morning with Jesus.

IN MEMORY

Frank Clark… our father. He loved Sunday brunch right after having attended Sunday mass … eggs, toast, warm coffee and a big bowl of fruit topped with a banana. He always said his special grace before each meal. Occasionally we went to "Pal's Pancake House" and he even said grace there.

Grace

May the blessing of the five loaves and two fish which Jesus divided among the thousand put luck on our food and portion. Amen

CONTENTS

SPECIAL MESSAGE: as you read, reflect and ponder the Good News of the Breakfast with Jesus sharings, you will notice some of them are short and some are long. It is the message they contain that is the blessing. Think of how the sharings resonate with your emotions ~~ perhaps you are inspired, challenged or feel that this is just a wonderful spiritual adventure to have with Jesus.

Chapters: The chapters in this book will not be titled or given a page number in the contents. The Authors invite you to open to a page anywhere and share . . . *Breakfast with Jesus*.

Look for surprise recipes spread throughout the book

DEDICATION

This book is dedicated to all those persons who serve breakfast so joyfully to people in hospitals, nursing homes, homeless shelters, special group homes and rehab centers. To all people who bring breakfast to those in need with a caring heart and spirit~~you truly are Jesus' presence of great compassion.

In particular... this dedication speaks about the World Central Kitchen (WCK) started by chef Jose Andres in 2010 to empower communities and strengthen economies by sharing food. This group has gone all around the world to countries in disasters and crisis... "to feed the hungry". I hope you will dream with WCK and envision a world where there is always a hot meal, an encouraging word and a helping hand in hard times... "in the breaking of the bread". For more information on this organization go to wck.org

Bread is...
        ...sustenance
        ...comforting
        ...nourishing
        ...life-giving

For some... bread is
        ...respect
        ...hope
        ...compassion
        ...forgiveness
        ...understanding

Bread... the "manna from heaven" is Love.
It is freely given... generously to all people

Let us...
Share our "manna from heaven" ...
        ...in ways God calls us to
        ...by being Jesus' love here on earth. Amen

PROLOGUE

Imagine... one day you wake up feeling very well rested and in unusually good spirits. You look out the window and see a bright shining sun and a beautiful blue sky. You open your back door and smile as you hear the birds chirping around the feeder. A gentle breeze allows you to breathe in the fragrance of the flowers in your garden. Silently you say a prayer of thanks for the gift of a new day. Just as you go back inside to make your 'much needed' cup of morning coffee, there is a knock on the front door. "Who could that be this early", you wonder. Before answering, you take a quick look in the mirror to make sure you look presentable. Then... there's another knock. Finally, you hurry to open the door. You're about to apologize that it took you so long to answer but... when you saw who your visitor was you froze and could not speak. Your eyes lock and His tender loving gaze touches your heart so much so that a tear trickles down your cheek. You are totally awestruck with the Presence before you. After a few seconds, which felt like hours, your mesmerized state was interrupted when He smiled and said, "Good morning, my name is Jesus. Would you like to have breakfast with me?"

In **Breakfast with Jesus**, Sister Ave and her co-author and brother Joe invite us to picture what it would be like to actually BE with Jesus, share a meal and have a conversation. What would you serve him? What would you talk about? What questions would you ask him? Why did he choose you when you are so unworthy? (Hello... we all are!!)   All these thoughts, and more, would be racing through your mind.

As you read through the sharings in the book, see which ones you can identify with... or maybe you would have a completely different breakfast planned. If that is the case, a blank page is included for you to write your own personal sharing. Also, be on the lookout for a few "holy" recipes scattered throughout the book for you to try... a Sister Ave surprise!

The painting on the cover, which was specially created for this book, perfectly reflects the intimacy the disciples had with Jesus. Take a moment to meditate on the words the artist used to describe the painting and what she hopes we all will see.   Just as the disciples met the resurrected Lord on the beach, let us meet him at our breakfast table, or anywhere, and allow him to minister to us, satisfy us and feed our hungry souls.

I was honored to be asked to write the prologue for this book. Sister Ave has been a blessing since I met her, especially since my retirement, by allowing me to be part of Heart to Heart Ministry. I am forever grateful.

Susan Schwemmer
Heart to Heart Friend

AUTHORS' NOTES

Just imagine... having breakfast with Jesus.   It would be a delight to serve him. I think he would accept whatever we each prepare for him. The important aspect of the meal would be our sharing from our hearts.

Do we listen?
Do we hear his call?
Do we understand that his love is always there for us?
What does Jesus say that touches our hearts?

Listen we do!
Heard his **calling!**
Unconditionally!
His compassionate words!

"Come and have breakfast ..."
(John 21:12)

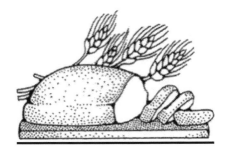

Breakfast with Jesus

(This poem leads us into the "spiritual" journey of sharing
Breakfast with Jesus…feeling his presence and taking the
grace of his words into our daily lived experiences.)

Breakfast ... it is said to be the most important of all meals
Our first food of the day, after the fast of the night
Emerging from our retreat, into a world of dreams
Having said our prayers for today
       and contemplating our hopes for tomorrow
Seeking the sustenance to satisfy our hunger
       and quench our thirst
Imagine as you approach your morning table…
Your altar of renewal
You see the Savior there waiting for you
What would that prayer of grace sound like?
What foods would you eat to enhance the experience?
What words or thought would you exchange to savor the
       moment?
To enlighten and inspire you to venture out to encounter
The challenges and opportunities of another day
After having shared **Breakfast with Jesus.**

By James Palmaro

(James Palmaro, a gifted poet with heart words written in
prose. He himself is disabled with blindness and sees the
world through his faith-lived.)

Bill Bosworth... a friend of my brother Joe

If I were to meet Jesus and ask him to share breakfast with me it would definitely be at my home. If he, however, wanted to dine elsewhere, I would go with him wherever he chose. If he comes to my house, I would serve him a regular American breakfast of eggs, toast, hash brown potatoes and whatever meat he might ask for. Whatever I serve him, he accepts it so graciously.

Our conversation at the meal would be the most important experience that I could ever imagine. In my prayer life, I usually do all the talking. Now that I am face to face with Jesus, I would either be dumbstruck and silent and just listen to him or I would again talk too much and not allow him a word in edgewise. I see he is very patient.

I would be totally overwhelmed by his sitting with me at the breakfast table. However, I would be profuse in thanking him for the home that he is dining in and for the family he is dining with. I would be filled beyond breaking with gratitude to him for all the blessings he has so abundantly given to me and my family. I would especially thank him for all the times he has carried me through difficulties and struggles in my life; most notable his helping us through the death of our son. I would thank him deeply for the gift of my son's life and his caring for him in his kingdom.

At this point, I would get up from the table and embrace him for his tremendous love for me and his friendship. Jesus went through horrible torture and death for me and every human who has ever lived or will live so that we have the gift of heaven. The phrase "thank you" is not enough to convey what I feel in my heart for this tremendous act of love for me and for all human kind. I would thank him for my life because unless we are born and exist, we won't have the possibility of eternal life and love in heaven.

I would not want this visit with Jesus to end but when it came time for parting I am hopeful he would say, "this is not a parting, this is just a momentary farewell until we meet again in the place I have prepared for you." Nothing in the world could ever exceed the joy that would be mine for this special visit of sharing and having the privilege of serving Jesus.

I would like to share my brother Joe's words ... "Bill, your thoughts are amazing. I know Jesus is a deep part of your life. Truly you are one of Jesus' disciples here on earth … Peace."
As I read Bill's sharing I could feel the strength of his faith and his reliance on God's presence in his life. An inspiration for all of us at breakfast for Jesus at Bill's home.

What did you learn from this sharing?

GOD IS PRESENCE

In **Breakfast with Jesus** you will experience the joys, surprises, heart-losses and questions shared about how <u>God is Presence</u>

God is Presence...
> ...in the listening
> ...in the caring
> ...in the savoring of the "bread of life" with
>   one another

God is Presence...
> ...in honesty and hope
> ...in the "walking with" one another
> ...in the humble journey of our lives

God is Presence...
> ...in the breaking of bread
> ...in human solidarity
> ...in the call to live our prayer

Send us Your Spirit, O Lord so we can feel your presence... and be your presence for one another

"in the giving and sharing of bread..."

Peg Franco... a wonderful heart to heart friend

I would invite Jesus to the beach in the early Summer because the air is cool and the breaking waves make a peaceful sound. We would share salmon fish cakes, fruit salad, rolls and coffee or tea.

I would thank Jesus for the blessings he has given to me and would speak about the glorious days at the beach... the sunshine, the warm soft sand, the cool water, the waves that come in and return in a continuous flow... always there like the gifts from God... peaceful, reassuring and never ending. The conversation would also include the life-giving features of the ocean... the fish, the other sea-life, sea plants... all gifts for us to use and enjoy. I would ask Jesus to hold my hand as we walked along the shore of my life.

Something that Jesus shares that touches my heart would be his continual presence in all of creation. In fact, he holds all of creation in his hand. You know the song, "He's Got the Whole World in his Hand".

He then says the next time he comes he will take me to breakfast to meet some of his friends... the poor, the lonely and those with any need. I tell him I will be their friend too. He blesses me and I feel his presence forever in my heart wherever I go.

You have just met in this sharing a very faithful person. Like Peg, let us dare to share our humble and grateful feelings with Jesus.

What did you learn from this sharing?

Kathy Sheridan…. Dominican Associate

I would invite Jesus to my home. When he knocks on my door I would greet him with the biggest hug and tell him how happy I am to see him. We would sit in my kitchen and I would serve Him Vermont coffee, French toast and orange juice.

I would talk about my family and friends and ask him to keep them well and safe. I would also talk to him about what is happening in the world today; the pandemic, people at the border, homelessness and how we are destroying the earth.

He would tell me how he loves me unconditionally and will always be with me in good times and bad. He tells me someday he will take me to his home in heaven… hopefully not too soon! When Jesus leaves he looks back smiling. I put my hands over my heart… he does the same.

You would feel so welcome at Kathy's table ~~ and you would get a hug also. The conversation would have lots of "caring" in it.

What did you learn from this sharing?

Two "homeless" men I bring food to each month

I asked these two men where they would have breakfast with Jesus. Both said they would take Jesus to a bench near the railroad where they waited for my delivery. They would share what I had in the bag for them… bagels, fruit and some homemade cookies.

They would tell Jesus they were homeless but trying to do odd jobs for people. One man said he would tell Jesus what he learned being homeless. The older man said he would cry with Jesus (I did not ask why). I asked them what Jesus would say to them. They both smiled at me said that Jesus would tell them he loved them.

As I was leaving one man asked where I would have breakfast with Jesus. I said I would like to join them on the bench near the railroad. They laughed and said, "Sure but don't forget the homemade cookies!" Jesus loves them and so do we.

These two gentlemen just happen to be homeless. They also help each other keep up their spirits… with dignity.

"Apostles" like these two men gave to Jesus their humble selves... a profound lesson.

What did you learn from this sharing?

Celeste Grillo... a wonderful giving heart

I would invite Jesus to breakfast everywhere I am. Breakfast is a source of strength and stability, refreshment and nourishment. I need Jesus to accompany me everywhere. During restful nights, I thank him for my peace. During nights of anxiety and regrets I invite Jesus to keep me calm. In the morning, my first thought is awareness of Jesus and gratefulness to him for the breath of life.

As Jesus and I start the day together, I serve him with the Sign of the Cross as I place my hand on our home bible. I trace the cross on my forehead, my heart and my lips. I need to be reminded at this early part of breakfast time to keep Jesus and all his teachings in my mind as I think and decide. On my lips as I speak to myself and others and in my heart as it beats through the day and as my heart reacts to all his children and all the events I encounter throughout the day.

Jesus and I chat about everything. The words are sometimes silent, only Jesus can hear them coming from my heart into his heart. Sometimes the words are loud out of desperation, worry, sadness, anger and confusion. Other times, I thank him on my knees for the graces and blessings he so richly pours out to me and my family and friends and to vulnerable persons. This conversation with Jesus lasts throughout the whole day!

Jesus speaks to me in loving ways. I feel him guiding me and reassuring me through the verses in holy Scripture that I may be reading. The verse just jumps out at me and

I try to write his message in my journal. Jesus sends me messages through people who may need love and who are hurting, who are physically ill, who are psychologically challenged, who are spiritually downtrodden and who may be acting unkindly or acting in seemingly mean, selfish ways.

Jesus urges me to not give up on them, to keep loving them, to keep being kind to them and to know that he forgives me even if I am not treating others as I should. Jesus reminds me that I have not walked every step with them, that I do not know exactly where they have been, nor do I know to where they are going or what they may be facing after our encounter. I will never understand everything about his children (we are all his children), but I can accompany them at the present moment and share my nourishment with them which I receive from my forever Breakfast with Jesus.

Jesus gives me the strength to rest from them a while, but then he grants me the fortitude to try to soften their hearts with a good deed or a soft response. I pray that Jesus will invite me into His Sacred Heart for our next forever breakfast together… into his heart that is forever strong, even though it has suffered pain and has scars of the cross in it. Jesus' presence of unconditional love will help me believe and strive to be a source of strength and hope for others who are suffering silently or suffering loudly. Jesus is right here on earth with me so I can pray that I can do his good will here on earth with all of His children. I pray to be his helping hands, his feet for the journey of caring and his heart of wonderful kindness to all.

I so loved having breakfast with Jesus. I look forward to it tomorrow and tomorrow and tomorrow. Help me to share it with all of your children today and all of the tomorrows you give me to share. Amen.

Celeste reminded us in a very human way that Eucharist in action is the best nourishment to share with one another.

Peace be to you Celeste!

What did you learn from this sharing?

Sister Eva Mazzetta, O. P. ... an artist

I would invite Jesus to my room, the inner center of my being. It is my "Emmaus" experience~~my encounter with the Lord. I serve him my love, my desire to be focused to hear what he says. Often times I offer my "poor self" which at times might be complete "emptiness".

We chat about the things that are closest to me both "within" and "without". Very often there is silence but if I listen with the "ear" of my heart he assures me that he will never leave me! He tells me he walks alongside me every day. I feel Jesus makes up for what is wanting in me with his special daily graces he shares with me.

The next time Jesus comes he will invite me to somewhere on earth for breakfast where someone needs a few moments to be listened to, to hear a word of encouragement, comfort and compassion and perhaps even to experience a shared "tear" of understanding someone else's pain... the agape of the Emmaus experience with Jesus.

As we listen to Sister Eva share her time with Jesus, we are touched by her sincere listening to Jesus so that she too could, in return, share a "tear" with someone else and be his love here on earth.

It's your best that counts. Jesus carries us...
without us even knowing it. Sister, you have
served all of us well!

> What did you learn from this sharing?

Dorothy Hickey... a Bayside neighbor and friend

I would invite Jesus to have breakfast at my house. He has blessed me with a wonderful marriage after my first husband passed at only 48. We have a lovely home here that I am sure Jesus led us to.

I would serve Jesus eggs... (yolks and all!). I would talk about my family... they are the world to me.

My hopes for my grandchildren... what is going on with my 4 sons and 2 step daughters. He knows I pray daily and that I put my trust in him since I cannot control things to what I think best. I ask him to keep guiding them and know that I care deeply for each one of them. I would confess my short comings and ask for patience and a stillness of spirit.

Jesus would tell me to keep loving. He doesn't give up on me and I certainly will not give up on him. He is teaching me to be just love.

The next time he comes he invites me to a beautiful garden for breakfast. Even though it is on earth, it reminds me of my grandparents and parents and my baby daughter who passed. The garden would remind me of heaven... everything beautiful and with a purpose and season. Jesus holds my hand. He is my holy link from the past... to the present and a future to share with love.

You might just say Dorothy took us to a breakfast with much love for Jesus. All of life has meaning… in the heart of love.

This sharing makes me think of the serenity prayer and Psalm 23... "that goodness and mercy shall follow you..."

What did you learn from this sharing?

Joe Clark... Sister Ave's brother

"I am with you always" (Matthew 28:20)

It was very early in the wee hours of the morning returning from New York from a very long emotional night. I had gotten lost returning from New York to my hometown, Denville, New Jersey. I prayed to Jesus to get me home safe; my wife called me and became my co-pilot. Arriving home, we talked of what was going on. A quick hug with Peggy, and a shower and I was back to New York.

During the drive into New York, I prayed harder and harder. A prayer was answered and JESUS WAS WITH ME (in the passenger seat). This was very early in the morning! Jesus was beside me in the car. He asked me to slow down. We'll arrive there safe and sound he tells me. She is not going anywhere until you see her.

This was my first of many breakfasts with Jesus. That morning he talked more to me than I to him. We didn't eat food. I shared my concerns and emotions for my sister. March 10, 2004, Sister Ave, my sister, was hit by a 120-ton runaway locomotive! For the next several months on daily trips to Elmhurst Hospital I thanked Jesus for being with me.

I have invited Jesus to my home inside and outside. I have introduced him to all my family and friends privately. I have shown him what we have created for him... gardens of thanks in our backyard. We talk of the miracles we have witnessed and the multiple blessings on us and our friends and others.

I have been invited many times to be with Jesus in various places and life events and I truly rejoice in his messages to me.

E Pluribus Unum (out of many one)

What can I say about this sharing... I thank Jesus for this wonderful, caring brother. I remember those early morning visits when he would appear at my hospital door and say what are you having for breakfast. I felt Jesus sent him to me. Now, I know Jesus came with him.

What did you learn from this sharing?

Sister Marilyn Breen, O.P. ... a **good** friend

I would invite Jesus to a place of love where others are welcome. I would serve him scrambled eggs and toast and decorate it as nice as I could.

I would chat about my different ministries over the years and tell him how much I loved each one of them. He smiles. Jesus would tell me to continue to do good. He blesses me and says, "I will always be with you."

Sister Marilyn is truly a woman of faith. The simplicity of her sharing comes from a mighty fine heart.

Sister Marilyn... I met you years ago. You
continue to be a prayer blessing
of faithfulness.

What did you learn from this sharing?

Traci Fantazzo-Koontz... Enrichment Director, Sisters of St. Dominic, Amityville, NY

I would invite Jesus to my favorite vacation spot, a small cottage in Southold and eat on the deck overlooking the lake and experience nature together. Why? It is the quiet, peaceful place where I learned to take time and be still and enjoy the sounds of the birds and the wind blowing through the trees. It's truly a magical place.

I will serve Jesus a breakfast quiche so that it can be made in advance and my attention can be spent focusing on our time together and not in the kitchen apart.

We would talk about how much people have changed over the years and his thoughts on the advent of technology and how it impacts everything and also what his message would be in today's society. Would it be different from what he originally preached?

What touches my heart is that he tells me that my path in life is serving a purpose to enrich the lives of others. When he comes again he takes me back in time when life was simple so I can experience ordinary goodness.

When I was with Jesus I felt validated and was deeply touched that I was chosen to be in his presence at breakfast. It made me feel so peaceful to open my heart to Jesus... I realize that I can do that every day in prayer.

Nature sings of God's goodness... so wonderful as Traci shared... to be still and know God's peace is right there.

What did you learn from this sharing?

Kelly Boger... my niece

I would invite Jesus to the Brewed Awakening Restaurant in Metuchen, New Jersey. This was the first breakfast place we found in our town after moving with our first son Aidan. The owner made us feel like family and let Aidan go behind the counter to choose his cookie after breakfast.

We would order waffles, eggs, and chocolate milk for Jesus. We think he and the children would enjoy that. We would share with Jesus about what happened the prior week and what our plans and dreams are for the future. We would thank him for all the blessings we have.

We have another son, Declan, and bring him to the Brewed Awakening. I think my children would be so happy to share breakfast with Jesus. We would thank him for completing our immediate family and for the support of our extended family.

Jesus shares his strength and patience with us which we all needed during this pandemic. He also shows us how to be kind, honest and humble. I am so grateful to be in Jesus company.

This was a wonderful sharing. A whole family got to have breakfast with Jesus. I think you might just say he is a special family friend.

Bless Kelly and Harry ~~ they have much
patience with their boys, raising them in a
very polite likeness of Jesus.
Love, Grandpa

What did you learn from this sharing?

Louis Tognan... a great parish scout leader for many years

I would invite Jesus to the usual place I eat breakfast... our cozy home kitchen. I would give Jesus what I usually have... a healthy breakfast of cheerios, milk and coffee. He smiles at the cheer on the cereal box in my kitchen.

We talk about many things but I really want to find out how much was truth and how much was left out or embellished here on earth. He shares that the truth sets us free. Jesus knows my inner thoughts and longings. I share a quote with him by James Baldwin: "neither love nor terror makes one blind... indifference makes one blind". He tells me to live the gospel not just read it.

He says he will be back. I look forward to learning more. I feel good about his sharings.

Louis is a very honest man... Jesus likes us to share how we are feeling. That is how we grow and bring hope to the world.

What did you learn from this sharing?

Denise Batistoni... a Mercy Associate

I would invite to Jesus to my kitchen. We would sit at my humble kitchen table. I would serve a simple breakfast. We would talk about the world he created and also heaven... the eternal home. He tells me, I am blessed and loves how I make arts and crafts for other people to make them happy.

The next time he comes we will go to a diner together and sit in a private booth where I can share some private thoughts with him. I know he cares deeply about me.

Jesus knows just what we like to do. He affirms our "ordinary" caring actions. He loves each one of us with an everlasting love.

What did you learn from this sharing?

Sister Valerie DaSilva, O.P. ... Upstate O.P.

Since I eat breakfast at the kitchen table where I can see the trees which surround the area I live in, it is the perfect place to pray and talk to Jesus.

All I can serve him is my presence and ask for his care and holy presence in my life as I do my work during the day.

Does he speak and say something special? At times, I wish he would. I do feel comforted and able to do the work he has asked me to do all my life; (teaching Theology in College) telling others about him... perhaps that is his way of talking to me.

Our visit is a quiet one. I am so grateful he stopped in for breakfast. To my surprise he is coming back. I am sure we will share a bit more on his second visit.

Jesus accepts us as we are... he engages our hearts and spirits. He shares the silence of divine love... that is where we grow spiritually.

Throughout the years, Sister Valerie has been there
for me, my family and my sister, Ave.
Love, Joe

What did you learn from this sharing?

Sister Fran Gorman, O.P. ... an O.P. with a compassionate heart

I would invite Jesus to breakfast at the Lindenhurst Diner on Merrick Road because we could have a nice meal in privacy. Since it is a diner, someone else would be serving him...I would recommend the pancakes...mmm so good!

We would talk about our parents and how we were blessed to have such loving people in our lives. We would then discuss the state of the world. I would ask him what he thinks we should do about anti-Semitism, racism, climate change and all the issues that humanity is dealing with here and across the planet.

Jesus reminds me that there are and will continue to be ups and downs in life but he is with us all the time. He encourages me to trust and have faith in his promises. I find myself folding my hands in prayer.

He then invites me to go back in time and have breakfast with his friends Mary, Martha and Lazarus. It is a delight to meet these wonderful people. They serve matzah and butter. How did they know that was my favorite? Jesus smiles as he enjoys his matzah.

Jesus would remind me that not only is he in my heart but he is present sacramentality as well. I would send him a thank you note and ask him to bring his mother the next time he visits. Jesus is there every day in a special way for each one of us.

Sister Fran and Jesus have a good conversation about the world and also about how faith will be there in every moment of life. Maybe it is a "graced moment" to think of Jesus' presence early in the morning at breakfast time.

I hope the pancakes were chocolate chip with
whipped cream! I would ask Sister Fran...
how can we be better in this world?
~~ less hate!

What did you learn from this sharing?

Classic Shortbread ... "short-__PRAYER__ bread"

Submitted by Joe Clark

Ingredients:

½ cup butter at room temperature.
1/3 cup powdered sugar un-sifted
¼ teaspoon of vanilla
1 cup of flour un-sifted

Cream the butter until light. Cream in the powdered sugar and vanilla. Now work in the flour. Knead the dough on an unfloured board until it is nice and smooth.

Spray the shortbread pan very lightly with a non-stick vegetable oil spray. Firmly press the dough into the shortbread pan. Prick the entire surface with a fork and bake the shortbread right in the pan at 325 degrees for about 30-35 minutes, or until very lightly brown.

Let the shortbread cool in its pan for about 10 minutes. Loosen the edges with a knife and flip the pan over onto a wooden board. If the shortbread does not come right out, tap one edge of the pan.

Cut the shortbread in individual serving pieces while it is still warm.

Let the pan cool before washing in the sink or dishwasher.

(Joe wraps each piece individually and shares them with neighbors. He tells me people say... "thanks for the short bread". Joe says add a "**prayer**" to your recipe.)

Linda Luberto... a teacher with a heart

I can't decide if I would invite Jesus to breakfast in my yard or to a favorite casual restaurant nearby on Jamaica Bay. The bar/restaurant is a bit hidden away and is right on the water. The breakfast menu is limited and simple, but it's a peaceful place, and I can envision Jesus sitting back and feeling very relaxed and comfortable there. I think he enjoys being near the water, since he gathered his fishermen friends by the Sea of Galilee and spent much time there. I guess I'd leave it to him to decide between dining by the sea or if he'd prefer to come to me right where I am at home, because I'd want to do what he wants.

If he was coming to my house, I think I would want to bring my family and friends (especially my granddaughters) over to be with him as well. In that case, I would serve baked French toast I'd prepare the night before, bacon, eggs, sausage, toast, and pancakes/waffles. I'd have a nice big platter of fruit with juice, coffee and a variety of teas. I'd be another Martha, though, busy serving, no time to talk or be with him myself. So, if he only wanted to be with me for breakfast, I'd have him come and visit me in my kitchen while I prepared some eggs and pancakes and whatever he wanted. Oh, I know he likes fish, so maybe I would have some bagels and cream cheese and lox on hand, just in case.

I hope I wouldn't just chatter away nervously and waste my time with him. I hope he would do most of the talking and that I could mostly listen to him and bask in his loving presence. I might ask him if I'm doing all the things I should be doing in my life or if there are things I should change. I'd want to know if I'm following the Father's will in my life. I'd like to ask him about heaven and Mother Mary and St. Joseph and some of the saints and my parents and friends who've gone before me. I'd ask him if there was anything I could do for him.

Maybe Jesus would tell me to slow down and enjoy being alive. Maybe he'd tell me to focus on him and the Father and the Holy Spirit and invite the Trinity every day into my heart and soul and mind… just as I'd invited him to breakfast. He'd say to not sweat the small stuff and to act more like Mary and Martha. He'd say the more I focused on God and Mother Mary and my home in Heaven, the more I would see God right here on earth in all his people and creation. He'd tell me to go to Mary whenever I needed help in finding him because she'd always lead me to him. He said no one really knows how much he loves and cares for them, and that if we did, we'd be happier and much more peaceful. Jesus says God the Father wills love, peace and unity on earth as it is in Heaven. He said the Holy Spirit is here to heal and strengthen us and make us whole so we should call upon him for help. Jesus asks me to focus on loving others the way he loves me.

The next time Jesus invites me to breakfast on earth I hope it will be away to somewhere beautiful and peaceful, like the French or Italian countryside, so we can enjoy each other's company in a beautiful setting. If we go back in time though, I'd really like to go with him to his home with Mother Mary and Jesus and St. Joseph, and have breakfast with them too. They are my favorite saints and I'd love to learn more about them. How lovely that would be! But I guess that will have to wait until Heaven.

Maybe for today, though, I'll just ask Jesus to come right now in spirit and sit on my couch with me and have a nice cup of coffee. We won't talk much, though. We'll just enjoy sitting quietly together. Every once in a while, we'll just look at each other and smile. We're happy to just be together. And that's more than enough... It's everything.

It is so wonderful when someone shares their faith. When someone like Linda says it's everything... it is everything, and more. Amen.

What did you learn from this sharing?

Lorraine Jayson... a South Carolina friend

I would invite Jesus to the beach at sunrise to watch his awesome handiwork emerge as the sun rose upon his creation of a brand-new day. I don't think he would need any kind of food to eat but I would bring wine and bread so that He could change them into His body and blood and we could celebrate the Eucharist together.

I don't know if I could speak at all, but if I could, I would ask him to forgive me for hurting him with my sins. I would thank him for his unconditional love and grace. I would thank him for the gifts taken for granted each day like the air to breathe, water to drink, food to eat, trees, flowers, birds, loved ones, angels...

My big question would be why so much suffering in the world? Hunger, violence, disease, hate... young children and the aged with things like cancer and dementia whose loved ones have to suffer along with them? At times in my life this question has caused me to lose faith. Yes, we live in a sinful world but weren't all the sins of humanity nailed to the cross with you? So then, why??

Of course, Jesus would tell me how much he loves all of us (even me) enough to die to give us a chance at eternal life. I know he would tell me to trust him with all my heart and that his grace is sufficient. He would tell me his ways are not our ways.

I would feel awestruck, honored, humbled, unworthy, grateful, protected, nurtured and loved.

I would invite him on his next visit into my home and heart and ask him to guide me each day to do his holy will. I would hope to say "see you soon!" (in heaven). I would just feel so fulfilled and blessed to have this special breakfast time with Jesus.

That question about "suffering" is one we all have asked at some point in our life. Just knowing Jesus is there to companion us is a "holy" comfort.

Reading the gospels and striving to live them sure
help us with our questions and ponderings.

What did you learn from this sharing?

Joan Kovacs and Monday Morning Centering Prayer Group in Minnesota

All four agreed the breakfast would be at a place in nature where all could appreciate the beauty of creation. Several of the Red Wing Parks in Minnesota were suggested. We decided it was important to be out and part of nature with a picnic breakfast.

What would we serve? The first response was "something simple", to which another responder said, "something special" ~~~ this is Jesus. Opinions continued to include a full Brunch menu… muffins, fresh fruit, eggs. And then, because it was Jesus, who would follow Middle Eastern traditions, there would be wine and to go with the wine, some cheese and crackers. A question was raised "coffee? regular or decaf".

What would we chat about with Jesus? Not a darn thing that is happening today! We would want to stay in his presence of joy and love. We would enjoy sharing the beauty of Minnesota nature with Jesus. We would all be deeply grateful for this wonderful time spent with him.

We all agreed that if Jesus came again we would just want to be welcome into his arms for a loving embrace. He would get one back from each one of us. This would be so peaceful... we would not want him to leave.

This sounds like such a nice place to be… you can feel the peace being shared. Just being with Jesus is a blessing… no words needed.

Joan Kovacs ~~
our pilgrim ~~ always sharing and shining

What did you learn from this sharing?

Danielle Sondgeroth... college student

Jesus and I would have a nice picnic in the park. Maybe we would go to Central Park or Union Square, somewhere I would take my friends. Before we go, we stop at a grocery store and pick out some snacks. We grab a bottle of wine to share, some cheese and crackers and some fruit.

We find a nice spot to sit in the shade under a wide oak tree and lay out a blanket on the ground. We remove our shoes and sit down, digging into our food and enjoying the lovely summer sun. The breeze begins to blow and Jesus sighs and smiles. He tells me about the wonders of God's creation, how the wind is something to be appreciated. We talk about the earth and all of God's creatures, plants and animals alike, and how we can begin to save the planet, Jesus notices that I start to get a bit worried and nervous while we're talking about climate change. He hands me some water and pulls me into a comforting hug. He tells me, "no matter what happens, I love you and I'm always here for you to keep you safe." I start to feel much better after this.

We lay down on our backs and look up at the clouds, finding shapes and figures among them and pointing them out to each other. I ask him about his life in Judea. What was it like? How is the world different today? He smiles and says, "people are people, no matter the time or place."

I begin sharing with him about my family struggles ~~ growing up with a single mother and not knowing my father until I was much older, dealing with difficult issues, and building close relationships with some family members… and Jesus shares with me, too. He comforts me and I feel so peaceful. We talk about perseverance and how no matter how dark everything can seem, there is always light somewhere. You just have to find that light, believe in it and cherish it.

We stay in the park until the sun sets and we both return home. Next time he invites me for pancakes at a small family-owned diner. We put quarters in the jukebox at the table and settle in with our big breakfasts. He gives me a task this time. Jesus tells me that I must remain kind and gentle to all on this earth, and I must keep love in my heart for all people, even when they are difficult to love. I promise him that I will always try my best to love all whom I come across, and that I will strive to be kind, no matter what. I feel so at peace with Jesus.

Isn't it wonderful the gift of unconditional love Jesus gives to each one of us. We can dare to stir this love into our daily encounters with other people.

I think going to a "park" and being with Jesus in nature is a wonderful place to commune with God.

What did you learn from this sharing?

Patricia Russo... Retreatant from Tabor Retreat Center

I would invite Jesus to my home and we would have breakfast on the porch. This way we could feel the cool breezes of the day.

I would serve him veges and eggs with some ricotta cheese. I would ask him what beverage he would prefer. I would have coffee brewing.

I think it would just be nice to sit quietly with Jesus... just being in his presence is so life-giving.

Jesus says he will come again... we could go to the shore or to a garden. I tell Jesus I will be happy to go to either place. He says we can have another quiet time together. This makes me so happy.

Being quiet... being still... is truly a blessing. It fills us with wonder, comfort and peace.

What did you learn from this sharing?

Christine Lyons... my niece

If I had the chance to have breakfast with Jesus, I would invite him to Easter at my parents' house. We have a tradition of serving an Easter breakfast instead of dinner and it is one of my favorite holidays. Serving breakfast is much less stressful than preparing a full dinner so the atmosphere is very calm and loving.

I picked my parent's house and this day because there is always a variety of food to choose from. This buffet style would help to lead into further discussion of what Jesus enjoyed the most as my personal favorite is the croissant French toast.

After enjoying the food, I would invite Jesus to spend some time on the back deck to enjoy the beautiful Spring weather and talk about a few things.

I would definitely want to know more about my grandfathers because I was not able to know them personally. I would probably ask Jesus for life advice and general support when I feel doubtful.

Lastly, I would thank Jesus for my many blessings. I think Jesus would respond lovingly to my questions and in some cases not provide answers... just reminders to have faith and be a good person. We would end our time together with a warm hug and an open invitation to spend more time together.

I can imagine Jesus having a croissant French toast and telling Christine~~"good choice." Isn't it wonderful to believe we can just sit down and be in the presence of Jesus' love?

Christine, you are a very good person
and fine daughter.
Love, Dad

What did you learn from this sharing?

Shawn Lyons... husband of my niece

Given the chance to have breakfast with Jesus, we would eat at the clubhouse of Augusta National Golf Club. We would eat steak and eggs, medium rare with grits. We would talk about golf as we looked out onto the green.

I would suggest we spend our time together playing a round of golf with my dad and grandpa to complete the foursome. We would talk about where to regain sight as a society because more often than not negativity weighs heavy and it seems like we are all in need of direction. I think Jesus would say not to lose faith in God, country and family. Jesus listens and then scores a hole in one! Amazing day!

Jesus is interested in what we do here on earth and also how we feel. He listens with his whole heart...something we all can do also.

Shawn, you keep the faith quite well
by the way you live.

What did you learn from this sharing?

77

Tina Moore... from St. Bernard in Brooklyn

This year has been totally different (COVID). My grandson gave me a 365-day calendar with the title "Jesus Calling" … it sits in front of me on my dining room table and he speaks to me each morning. So, I guess that is where I will invite Jesus.

I would serve him anything he would like but he is welcome to all that I have. I usually give him all of my troubles and thoughts for the day. I always thank him for all my blessings. We usually talk about my kids and their families and how troublesome the world is today.

I tell him I want to come home but I am willing to wait for when he is ready for me. I always ask him to walk beside me as I go about my daily chores. Jesus always tells me to place my trust in him and not to be afraid. Today he actually told me to live by faith and not by sight.

Jesus invites me all the time to breakfast with him when I meet him at Mass each morning. He invites me because he loves me and wants to share himself (The Bread of Life) with me. I truly am so happy for his invitation… I feel so peaceful.

Like Tina, let us all live and walk with our Faith in all the events and experiences of life. This will bring us peace of mind, heart and spirit.

Whatever age your grandson is ... **Hoorah**!

What did you learn from this sharing?

Harriet Scott... holy lady from Saturday Phone Prayer Chat

I would invite Jesus to a diner in the South. We would have flapjacks with butter and maple syrup, hush puppies, thick bacon, two eggs over easy, orange juice and cups of coffee. While we ate, I would thank him for coming.

I would ask Jesus at this point in time what did he think of man's progress around the world... with the way we treat the environment, our communities, the rights of others, even our families and ourselves.

I am sure he would respond in parables, instead of just stretching out his arms and saying let there be peace and understanding worldwide. I would feel inspired and hopeful that tomorrow mankind would follow God's mandate to make this a better world and truly follow God's words... to love one another and live the 10 commandments.

When the Lord returns... he takes me to Greece in a café overlooking the sea with my 4th grade friend Irene. She has journeyed with me for 76 years. The Lord knows that our families rode the crest of celebration and tragedy together. We would enjoy the warmth of his goodness. I would love to share seeing the face of Jesus with her. I would hope to see a better world for all God's people. Jesus smiles and says... do all in my name.

Think of a friend who has been with you on your life's journey. Remember… Jesus is your friend, always by your side.

What did you learn from this sharing?

Vito and Tony... from Barney's Service Station, Bayside, NY

Vito -- I invite Jesus to the beach to see the vastness of creation

Tony -- I invite Jesus into my heart

Vito -- I serve him fruit… a symbol of his bounty

Tony -- I serve him love and happiness

Vito -- We chat about Life Everlasting

Tony -- We chat about peace on earth

Vito -- I tell him I would love to hear about my departed loved ones

Tony -- We share about eternal life in heaven

Vito -- the next time Jesus comes he is going to take me to the United Nations Peace Summit to show me that peace is the way to live.

Tony -- the next time Jesus comes he is going to take me to the Holy Land.

You know where you find God… everywhere. Well, I found God's wonderful kindness in Tony who owns Barney's Service station with his best pal Vito by his side. Over the years I have gotten bills with a smile and best of all… an example of how they respect everyone and treat their workers. Think of people who reflect the goodness of God in the world.

What did you learn from this sharing?

"Give us this day... our daily bread..."

What does that mean ...
    ...to people who lost their home in a fire
    ...to children in a garbage dump looking
        for scraps of food
    ...for someone who lost a loved one
        during this pandemic
    ...for someone who is unemployed
    ...for someone who lives daily with a scar of
        trauma

What does it mean to have daily bread?
We pray in the prayer... Our Father
"Give us this day... our daily bread..."

What are you praying for?
What am I praying for?

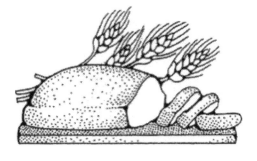

Earline Brown… holy lady from Saturday Phone Prayer Chat

I would invite Jesus to share breakfast at a homeless shelter, where the homeless persons and I can be fed by Jesus with food that nourishes our souls too.

I would also invite Jesus to come sometime to have breakfast with me at my kitchen table where we can together look out my glass door and see God's peaceful dark blue sky. It is there that I feel God's presence many times. Jesus smiles at me.

I would serve him my homemade bread and offer him some grape juice with it. Jesus told the disciples, "Do this in memory of Me..." This for me would commemorate the Last Supper and Jesus request… I strive to do his will here on earth by helping others.

I would discuss with Jesus how I could better live more in ways that are pleasing to God: bless the lowly with kindness, humility, service and love; guiding others in love and faith in Jesus Christ Our Lord by the way I live; follow God's plan and purpose for me; how to help make the world a better place for all people to live. All these done with a sincere heart.

I would be touched if Jesus told me he felt love in my heart. As I look out my kitchen glass door tomorrow, I know he is right there with me. Now I smile.

When we look out into life...Jesus is right there encouraging and affirming each one of us. Look up at the beautiful dark blue sky and be reminded Jesus is right there by your side.

What did you learn from this sharing?

Two sisters... Josephine (Jo) and Julie

We would invite Jesus to our home and offer him a variety of breads, muffins and toast. We would chat about family. It makes us happy that the Lord is always with us. Just like we suffer at times, the Lord has suffered for all of us. He understands.

The next time he comes he goes to church with Julie. They celebrate His love there by praying together. And for Jo, He takes her to a view of her past… showing her all the ways she followed his love.

Two sisters, who have been there for each other in the ups and down of life put their Faith into action by their wonderful caring for each other… sharing tears and joys and just being wonderful "sisters". How do you put your Faith into action?

> What did you learn from this sharing?

Vito DiBona... wonderful friend and computer helper

I would take Jesus to a wonderful Bagel Shop where I would suggest that he get the "everything bagel". It has a variety of seeds.

I would feel that I could ask him about everything in my life. He tells me that all will be fine... this makes me feel good.

Just being with Jesus makes me feel secure about life. The next time He comes, we will be outside in nature and enjoy the beautiful scenery and wildlife. He tells me it will be so peaceful. I am so grateful for all the Lord has done for me.

Next time you get a bagel...try the "everything" bagel! That made me smile and it also reminded me that everything is blessed by God.

> What did you learn from this sharing?

Pearl Grisham... holy lady from Saturday
Phone Prayer Chat

I would invite Jesus to my humble home. I would serve him pancakes and eggs. I would ask him to give me more Faith and Wisdom. I would also ask him to help me hear the Father's voice when he speaks to me.

I would listen to Jesus quietly and reverently. He tells me that the Father is with me all the time. I just have to believe with all my heart and never stop trusting. I know he will come back again.

It is so wonderful to reflect on each sharing… hmmm, we can ask the Lord for anything. What do you ask the Lord for?

What did you learn from this sharing?

Mary Cesare... minister of bereavement

I have thought long and hard about this wonderful event and I have finalized my thoughts. Based on Scripture, we know Jesus loves fish. He asked for it after the Resurrection to prove he was not a ghost, or just the apostles' imagination and he made a fish breakfast on the beach for the apostles when they were out fishing.

So, my breakfast would be smoked salmon (lox) with onions and challah bread, a large bowl of fresh fruit cut in pieces... watermelon, strawberries, blueberries and cantaloupe. And of course, a large mug of good black coffee. He loves coffee.

I make the breakfast and sometimes serve it on the sun porch, but most of the time at the kitchen table. Jesus likes it there best. The one question I always ask him is: "why in God's name would you die for me? I'm not worth it." And his reply is always the same. "You answered your own question. It was for the name of God."

After that we talk about the weather, what I could do for him that day and the mess the world is in because we aren't seeking his help. He doesn't like speaking about politics now any more than when he was on earth 2000 years ago. Sometimes I ask silly questions like who sits on the left hand of God the Father. You're on the right, who's on the other side? Abraham, Elijah, Moses, Mary?

At other times the questions are deeper and more personal questions like when I was very sick 2 years ago, why did you let me live~~why, what am I to do now? I listen Lord, but I haven't gotten an answer yet. Jesus listens to me as He drinks his coffee. He smiles with wonderful compassion. Perhaps the answer lies within my heart of faith as I join the Ministry of Consolation group at my church and share God's love with people who have experienced the loss of a loved one.

When Jesus finishes his coffee, He smiles with such tenderness and says that He will be back again and without another word He gently leaves. When he does return I will ask him if we can share breakfast on a boat, at dawn, on the Sea of Galilee. As I write this I'm looking at a picture of the Sea~~a very peaceful and heavenly place. Something tells me he will have fish for me on a warm fire by the sea. I can't wait!

Jesus' very presence communicates love and kindness. We can go to Jesus anytime and anywhere… he is always there to listen to our heart sharings.

What did you learn from this sharing?

Linda Mercer... holy lady from Saturday Phone Prayer Chat

I would invite Jesus for breakfast on the beach. I would have a feast for Jesus of fresh fish, bread, plenty of fruit and vegetables. We would chat about all the blessings he has given me, all the love he has shown me.

I would apologize for the many times I was weak, faithless and wouldn't wait on him. I remember the countless times the Lord carried me. He reminds me that he is my rod and staff. I am overjoyed with his presence in my life.

When Jesus comes again to take me to breakfast, he shows me that he is not selfish... he invites all my brothers and sisters, grandparents I have never met and aunts and uncles who have gone before me. He also invites neighbors, enemies, the sick, sad, anxious, unhappy, depressed and homeless persons.

He takes me back to the beach where there is plenty of room for everyone to eat. He shares his love unconditionally with each one of us. He shows us how we can treat each other. My heart is so full of love.

Linda's sharing opens our hearts to what **Breakfast with Jesus** is all about:

> ...being a presence of love
> ...include everyone in your life
> ...serve one another with compassion

What did you learn from this sharing?

Daniel... Bayside Farm Deli, he serves with great joy!

I would invite Jesus to have breakfast with me at my house. The reason I would invite Jesus to my house is because I would feel much more comfortable and open my heart to him there.

The food I would serve to Jesus is some salmon with some fresh squeezed lime, vegetables, a bowl of fruits and nuts and perhaps a cup of tea.

I would chat with Jesus about my life and also how to forgive myself for any wrong I had done. Jesus smiles and says I love you. This makes me feel comforted and very happy.

The next time Jesus says he will come for breakfast, he will take me outside in nature where we could sit and share even more.

When I get on line at the deli counter in Bayside Farms, I look for Daniel just to wave and see his smile. To me it is the smile of Jesus love serving others. Who do you know that has the smile of Jesus?

> What did you learn from this sharing?

Laura Clark... my nephew Bill's lovely wife

I would take Jesus to the hockey rink and have a nice warm cup of coffee and donut for Him. Jesus and I would watch my son John play hockey. I notice Jesus watches the game intently. He turns to me and says, "John is one good player". I ask him to watch over and protect my wonderful son. Just before he leaves he blesses me and says, "I love your little family. I'll be back for the next game too!"

Well now you know Jesus likes hockey! He enjoys how we share love with family.

Please watch over this wonderful family!
Love, Grandpa

What did you learn from this sharing?

Bill Clark... my nephew (godson too!) and
a marine veteran

I would take Jesus to Iraq... where I served with my brother marines. I would serve him an MRE meal (meals ready to eat). Why this meal? To show him this is how we ate while in Iraq. I would tell him that there is no bond stronger with another marine than one forged in common service.

I would tell him that those who paid the ultimate sacrifice for the greater good are never forgotten and held in high regard. Jesus listens with great love. I say it is now our job to honor them and to live our lives in the best way and to cherish every second here on earth. Jesus nods solemnly.

I would also tell Jesus that his own sacrifice for us has continued to be a great lesson... to teach us all that to sacrifice for what we believe in can inspire peace and hope for all.

Sometimes it is in the sharing of our life journeys ...that we can feel God listening to our very soul and spirit.

Special son... his nickname is "the major" and wherever he goes he champions the situation... as he said in his breakfast chat. Thanks Bill for the clear advice in *marine* talk. "I copy that!"
Love, your Dad

What did you learn from this sharing?

Jim Yhap... is studying to be a Deacon

I would invite Jesus to the very best restaurant. Many times in scripture he dined with wealthy people... to teach them a new way.

I am not wealthy and am unemployed right now but I will find a way to take my Lord to the very best restaurant, even if I have to borrow from someone.

I know Jesus loves seafood. I will make sure the meal is the very best Mediterranean diet with bread and fine wine. We will finish up with a nice cup of tea and good dessert... perhaps a delightful yogurt treat. Jesus loves to break his bread and share it. I say thank you.

I will love to listen to his precious words and will ask permission to record them. I will also have pen and paper to takes notes as a backup. I don't want to miss anything he says. He tells me about scripture and clarifies some passages for me.

If he prefers me to do most of the talking I am happy to listen first... then bring up what I usually tell him on a daily basis: to give grace to those in need, who feel neglected, to let peace prevail in our world, not hatred or violence and to be there for all families feeling some stress or loss.

I would also ask him where he is calling me to go and what specifically would he like me to do for him. I would share with him how hard discernment is for me at times.

He speaks with such kindness and tenderness and tells me all my good deeds reflect the love of his sacred heart. I feel so peaceful being with him. He wraps the extra bread for me and says, "I bet you will share this". "Yes, Jesus", I say.

The next time he comes he takes me to the humblest of places... perhaps on the seashore as the sun is rising where the small waves lap softly against the shore. We will sit on rocks, and listen to the crackling of the firewood roasting the fish and feeling its warmth.

He invites the hungry fishermen over and introduces them to me. He says, "This is Jim he is a Deacon. I am so proud of him." They all clap for me and I realize I have just made some new friends. In this humble place I thank Jesus for showing me the way.

As you read this sharing I truly believe you can feel the deep love Jim has for Jesus. We find our way very often when we let Jesus lead us.

Bless you, Jim. Despite any difficulty you keep on in life. Jesus is right there... and all our prayers for you.

What did you learn from this sharing?

Dr. Paul Clark, M.D. ... my older brother

I would invite Jesus to breakfast at a kindergarten class I tutor in reading. I think I would just watch. He calls the children his young disciples. The Lord shares and cares to listen to the children. He smiles quite often during the visit.

As he leaves, I tell the Lord I see him more clearly through the eyes of the little children. He turns and blesses them… then me.

Interesting... not so much about what was served… but who was there.

... from a Doc's "heart"

What did you learn from this sharing?

Mary Morris... a Dominican Associate

One early morning, the Lord knocked at my door and I invited Him in for a breakfast of cheerios, blueberries, diced peaches, milk and lots of tea.

As we sat at the kitchen table a conversation slowly began. He asked how I was and how things were going. I replied "fine". He just looked at me with a slight smile on his lips and a tilt of his head. Seeing that, I quickly added, "well, maybe not so fine but maybe not so bad either." We both had a hearty laugh together and that was the ice breaker for me.

We talked about my concerns for family, friends, country and the world. We talked about my loves, fears, doubts and joys but most of all Jesus listened. He listened to all my ramblings even to the ones I know didn't make much sense or simply were not kind. He never interrupted or rebuked me. He simply accepted all that was on my heart or at least what I could think of at the moment.

When he stood up to leave, he placed His hands on my head and said, "Peace be with you. Know that my love and forgiveness are yours." Alleluia! Alleluia! What joy filled my heart.

When we next visit, the time and place is up to him. I look forward to sharing this adventure with him. Wherever we end up, I only know that with Jesus by my side I am safe.

You know, after reading Mary's sharing, I could feel Jesus hand upon my head reminding me that no matter what is happening in life, he is right there. Close your eyes and you might just feel the presence of God encouraging you too.

What did you learn from this sharing?

Irene Mays... holy lady from Saturday Phone Prayer Chat

I would invite Jesus to breakfast under a tree by a peaceful lake where his flowers bloom. I would serve him bread and wine (to receive His blessing) then I would add blueberries, melon and an omelet with a pretty napkin with a nature scene on it.

Jesus explains his gift of creation to me and His unconditional love for me. I learn to truly listen. I ask Jesus to help me to be what He has created me to be. He puts His hand over His sacred heart and I lean on Him in peaceful silence.

Jesus tells me the next time he comes to visit me he will take me to His garden or back to the beautiful tree. I invite my partner so that we can bond together in giving praise, glory and thanks giving to Jesus and receive his blessing together. We will both be awed by Jesus' presence, mercy and grace. Listening to his wisdom leads us to a good sacred pause in our life. Cannot wait for that visit... so much to prepare and talk about the next time Jesus comes to breakfast.

You can almost see Jesus sitting under the tree of life. His very presence in our hearts stirs new life within us. Just imagine yourself leaning on the heart of Jesus's love every day.

> What did you learn from this sharing?

Theresa Harris... was a principal and worked at homeless shelter

Some food I would consider serving Jesus are bread and fish. I might even offer some chicken. I'd ask who he would like to invite to join us.

After the meal, I would like to sit and listen to his thoughts and kind wisdom. We could mention and discuss family members and friends. I'd hope he would give me some suggestions and solutions.

I would tell him if there was anyone needing some encouragement I would be willing to help them in any way possible. He smiles at me with such tenderness.

When escorting Jesus to the door, I would thank him for coming and invite him to return anytime. The welcome mat is always out for him. I would even give him lunch or supper if he liked. I would invite some friends and neighbors over so they could meet him too.

Going to bed, I would thank him in my prayers for his miracle visit. As I put the light out, I felt a glow of love in my heart.

How nice that Theresa wants to share her visit with others. Believe me the welcome mat at her home is her beautiful smile.

A warm smile of hospitality... just like Jesus!

What did you learn from this sharing?

Sister Pat McCann, O.P. ... Member of Peony Set

I will pray with Jesus in my room with a cup of coffee. I serve Jesus the best thing I have and that is my love! In my prayer with Jesus, I ask him to watch over my words and actions. I ask him to help me to grow in his love so that I may become a reflection of his goodness to others.

He seems to tell me to keep on doing what I am doing and that he is always with me. I believe the place that Jesus will invite me the next time he comes will be to go to church together. It is there at Mass, especially at Communion time, that I can be intimately united with him. Jesus tells me that he is with me in my every prayer. Perhaps that is why I love my quiet morning prayer time and cup of coffee to start my day off.

Good Morning God!   That cup of coffee and morning prayer can be a very special time that sets the tone for the day. Let us Pray as Sister Pat does... and serve Jesus our love.

Good Morning God! Keep serving your love,
Sister Pat ~~ sounds wonderful! I will too.

What did you learn from this sharing?

Sister Ellen Smith, RSM... Mercy Sister

I would invite Jesus to the beach on a cool day. The breeze would remind me of the spirit of caring Jesus brings with him. I would serve him homemade scones, warm coffee and some dates and figs. Jesus and I would have a serious discussion about the earth and how human beings are destroying it. Jesus wants us to care for creation.

He speaks to my heart and says that I can help to save the planet by my example. I will follow his advice by speaking about climate change to people and seeing how in our small actions we can help. The next time Jesus comes he takes me on a trip to see an iceberg that is ready to break up because of climate change. He is reinforcing in me the need to be pro-active now. I appreciate the earth and universe he gave us. I tell him I am full of gratitude for his message to care for the earth. He blesses me next to that melting iceberg. I will never forget his words of blessing.

Let us all take note that Jesus calls each one of us to care for the gift of the earth. Let us, like Sister Ellen, become better stewards of the environment.

Climate change is real... read Genesis.

What did you learn from this sharing?

Jesus Mini Waffles of Love
Submitted by Susan Schwemmer

Ingredients:
½ cup butter, softened
1 cup sugar
2 large eggs, room temperature
1 teaspoon vanilla extract
1 ½ cups all-purpose flour
1 teaspoon baking powder and salt
½ teaspoon salt
Confectioners' sugar

Beat together butter and sugar till fluffy. Add eggs and vanilla till thoroughly combined. Combine flour, baking powder. Mix into butter/sugar mixture.

Drop by heaping tablespoons full onto hot waffle iron. Sprinkle with confectioners' sugar.

Store extras in plastic baggies or containers to keep fresh.

"... no one is born a great cook~~you learn by doing."
(Julia Child)

Lillian and Anthony Merola… and Dad

(Dad) I would share with Jesus my favorite breakfast of a fresh orange, cheerios or oatmeal. We would sit at my kitchen table. I would thank him for the gift of music. Jesus knows I played the trumpet for Anthony's birthday in April. Jesus tells me my playing has brought so many people great joy. He winks and says, "You are a good trumpet player". I tell Jesus just being with him today is a gift. He says he had such a good time he will come again for breakfast and listen to me play the trumpet. This makes me really happy (that means I am still alive!)

(Anthony) I will invite Jesus to the International House of Pancakes since he is the King of Kings and Lord of Lords… of the world. I will serve him the finest hospitality... Love and Praise... the waiters and waitresses do the rest by bringing good food and a big stack of pancakes. We would talk of the need for Peace on earth with family, friends, neighbors and strangers. Jesus shares that peace is for everybody. Everything he says is so special. He tells me the next time he comes we will go to a baseball game and have Breakfast with the "Bombers" … the NY Yankees! He says he has a Yankee hat! Anthony says… we saved the best for the last.

(Lillian) I would invite Jesus to our sweet Brooklyn home. I would serve him some toasted bagels with cream cheese. I would serve him good coffee and we would have a chat about our families and the world. I ask him how we can be good shepherds. He tells us to always care for those with any need. We listen tenderly and will always remember his presence in our lives. Jesus says next time he will take all of us to my son's home to see the grandchildren. We will have pancakes with lots of blueberries on them. Jesus knows we all love blueberries. I tell Jesus I love him with all my heart and so does Anthony and his dad. Jesus says, "I love you too with all my heart." This was just the best day ever.

Jesus is family-oriented. He calls each of us brother and sister. I would imagine Jesus enjoyed being with the grandchildren... and the blueberries too!

What did you learn from this sharing?

Susan Pussilano... book cover artist and Heart to Heart friend

I would invite Jesus to my house because my kitchen table is so comfortable and hospitable. Many conversations, disagreements, plans, joys and sorrows came to be in that place. It was real with life.

I would serve my Lord something simple for breakfast yet nourishing and delicious like baked oatmeal. I remember his words to Mary and Martha. I would so much love to be Mary!

I would want to know all the things about heaven that are not written in the bible. I would ask Jesus about my husband Phil and my parents and loved ones. I would want to know how incredibly whole, healed and complete they all are now.

I would ask Jesus to tell them how much I miss them and how my heart aches for Phil but that I am doing wonderful here this side of heaven "with the Lord and by his amazing grace".

Jesus would share his unconditional love for me and grace me with another measure of understanding of his wisdom, his forgiveness and his everlasting love.

He tells me he will come again for breakfast and will invite me to the edge of his life and allow me a glimpse of what eternity with Him will be like. THAT would be dessert of course!

Susan let us know Jesus understands the aches in our heart
even as we keep on with life each day. Perhaps that visit at
the edge of greatness is something for all of us to ponder.

I would also like to experience going to the
edge of his life and get a glimpse of
eternity ~~ got it in your sharing!

What did you learn from this sharing?

Sister Peggy was in Puerto Rico for a special celebration visit. While there she and some sisters enjoyed sitting and sharing about **Breakfast with Jesus** questions. Here are the sharings of the sisters:

Sister Ida Negron, O.P. -- I would ask Jesus what he would like to eat. When speaking with him I'd talk about what's going on in the world today. I would be very interested in what he thought of current events. He would tell us all to "Keep Going". I would nod my faithful Yes, Lord.

Sister Ana Maria Androver, O.P. -- I would invite Jesus to my favorite place...Casa Familia where the children are. I would serve him coffee, ham and cheese. I would then ask him if He would like to stay for lunch also. I want to know what he thinks of the violence and unrest in the world these days. Jesus looks at me with hope. He says, "Te amo I love you, be with the poor." He would remind me of the story of the 10 bridesmaids ..." be ready"
In my heart I feel I am here Lord... to share your love.

Sister Providencia Perez Rodriguez, O.P. -- I would make eggs sunny-side up, bread and strong coffee. We'd talk about the world today. "Dios Mio!"

Sister Zaida Gonzalez, O.P. -- I would ask Jesus to come to my home. I would prepare scrambled eggs, some od local baked bread and coffee with milk. No more COVID please, Jesus. We need a miracle!

Sister Peggy, O.P. -- Prioress of Amityville Dominican Sisters -- I would share my Hershey bar and diet soda with Jesus and tell him about the wonderful hospitality and sense of mission that our sisters in Puerto Rico are living each day. I would just listen to what he would say to us. Jesus says to me… "mi courazon, mi vida, mi amor!" My heart, my life, my love! What a blessing to share that message. Glad we all had breakfast with Jesus.

All the sisters wanted to share with Jesus about the conditions of the world especially during this pandemic. They all look to Jesus for guidance to follow his call to serve with great love especially to those in need. Perhaps he is showing us how to be the Good News in a "wounded" world. (Since this sharing, Sister Ida Negron returned to the Lord. I am sure when she arrived in heaven the Lord shared his eternal Yes with her).

We all have this common ground...how to adapt to
current events in better ways. Sisters, you are
true examples of Jesus' love

What did you learn from this sharing?

Matt Romero... a truck driver from Colorado

Well, nothing fancy for breakfast just plenty of love from my heart. I think he might like some eggs and warm vegetables as a side dish.

I would chat about the rough life I have had and tell him I appreciated so much all his caring and love for me despite any hardships I was experiencing. Because of his great understanding heart, I learned to trust the Lord more. I feel comfort in his Sacred Heart.

The Lord tells me he was there in all those tough times and saw how I struggled. I held on with my faith. He says he loves me and sends his peace every day. He also says that is why he sent Sister Ave and Heart to Heart Ministry into my life. I tell Jesus that Sister and I have nice chats on the phone while I'm driving my truck and that she is great company with her sense of humor. I tell him that when our conversation ends I say, "God Bless You Pearlbud".

As Jesus gets ready to leave me He says, "Peace be to you", and I wave. He says he will meet me at another truck stop in the near future. I feel at peace.

Back some years a truck driver named Matt called me and said he had my card and would it be OK if he called me now and then. We have had wonderful conversations about faith over the years. I love being called "Pearlbud".

Matt has great faith in his heart!

What did you learn from this sharing?

Sister Alphonse Louise Gendron, O.P. ...
a praying heart

I would take Jesus to a diner. The prices are not extravagant. He will get a large portion of whatever he likes to order and he will even have some leftovers to take home. We talk about ordinary things and whatever else we chat about I feel whatever he says is so special and meaningful for me to hear. The next time he comes we will go to the same diner. We both agreed this was a pleasant place to come to have breakfast. As he leaves... he looks back and waves... so do I with a big smile. I feel so blessed to have this special time with my Lord, Jesus.

Isn't it wonderful to be able to chat with Jesus about "ordinary" things. Jesus enjoys companioning us on our earthly journey.

St. Peter likes leftovers! Very often the
leftovers feed others.

What did you learn from this sharing?

Louise Mendenhall... sincere heart friend

I would invite Jesus to my home as this is where I am comfortable. I would serve him warm oatmeal with a banana or fried eggs and toast. I would let him choose what he would like to eat.

I would apologize for the plain food but he reassures me that the food is quite good and very nourishing. He says he has had enough of fancy food for a while... this makes me relax.

We have a nice conversation. At one point there are tears in his eyes as he tells me how he wishes I could appreciate all the good I do. He wishes I could feel how much he wants to help me. I tell him I will practice his advice a bit more. His gentle voice is so affirming.

He tells me the next time he comes for breakfast he will take me to the seashore. I love the story of John 21 because he provides a charcoal fire with fish and bread. Then he says, "come have breakfast". I feel honored that the Lord came to my home. As he leaves he points to the table. He left me a note. After he leaves I read it and hold it over my heart. It says, "thank you for a delicious healthy breakfast. You are my beloved... keep serving the Lord with your wonderful kindness."

In this sharing Jesus shares tears… isn't that something? He shows how much he cares about Louise… us too.

What did you learn from this sharing?

Sister Laura Helbig, O.P. ... a "joy-filled" O.P.

I would begin my day with Jesus at Mass. It is a holy opportunity to put my gaze of my first greeting of the day on the Lord, Jesus. I would give him all the intentions I have in my heart for others.

Serving Jesus is easy because he is ever so grateful for all we do for one another in all the ways that life provides through him. I usually serve a good deal of thanksgiving for all he provides me with during the day that will serve others in need with much love.

Then I usually serve large portions of faith and hope that will enable those in need to receive from their loving neighbors. Oh yes, I ask him to bring some forgiveness for the times I neglected to listen to his nudges and opportunities to express his love here on earth in better ways.

We chat about my family, my Amityville Dominican congregation and all I love who are in some need of his healing, forgiveness and encouragement. I have been asking Jesus about this pandemic and when will we get back to some normal time... or is this the new normal? He is encouraging and asks me to be more aware of the good as well as the pain that has come as a result of this harsh reality. The two of us chat about all the suffering in the world around us and the moral and spiritual actions needed to address them.

Everything Jesus has shared with me... it is like the scriptures have come alive in word and spirit in me. In thinking about where he might invite me for breakfast the next time, it would seem to me he might just come back and be with me heart to heart again. Thank you, Jesus.

You can tell with Sister Laura that her time with Jesus was heart to heart. Perhaps we can all do this a little more each day... at breakfast time... and anytime.

What did you learn from this sharing?

Roma O'Hara... Divine Mercy Group

I would invite Jesus to have breakfast in my living room as it is comfortable there. I would serve Jesus Breakfast Blend coffee or Irish Breakfast tea (which ever Jesus prefers and the way he likes it), Greek yogurt with honey and a toasted hearty natural bread with creamy butter or a good jam (which ever he prefers).

I would chat about my love for him and what we are going to do together today. Jesus tells me to continue to persevere in prayer, not to worry... to trust him, be of good courage and to do good for others. This makes me feel peaceful.

Jesus says the next time we meet for breakfast it will be with him at the Holy House of Loreto, which is in Italy. He lived there with Mother Mary and St. Joseph. It is like Jesus is sharing his home me.

It seems Roma is giving Jesus some nice options for breakfast. Jesus does that in life for us... we get to choose what is good.

What did you learn from this sharing?

Monica Callender... Brooklyn Disciples in Mission Leader

I would invite Jesus to my home in Brooklyn. My daughter Lois and I will serve him bacon, eggs and toast and some nice coffee. We will sit quietly just being ever so happy that Lord came to our table.

We chat about the Holy Spirit and all the gifts the Spirit shares with us so we can be peace-filled and to share this peace with others.

He tells both of us that he loves us and is so happy how we gather people at retreats and scripture days of prayers. We bow our heads as he blesses us.

He says the next time he will take us to the seashore. He tells us this is where he met his first disciples. I look forward to that visit. I love watching the waves in the ocean. It reminds me of the gospel story where Jesus calmed the waves.

After he leaves we are both quiet... probably thinking of how his presence was encouraging, affirming and filled with profound love.

It sounds like Monica and her daughter Lois will long remember that visit at their table... so will Jesus!

Monica ~~ you have the spirit! Women are wonderful, holy disciples of Jesus.

What did you learn from this sharing?

Judy Bosworth... Joe's friend, Bill's wife

A knock is heard. "Who is it," I ask. "Jesus," he says. I think I know the voice. Another, softer knock. I throw open the door. There is a man standing on my doorstep. He says, "Now do you recognize me?"

Do I recognize him?!! I am on my knees with joy! Jesus at my door? How can this be? So, of course, I invite Him in. It's early enough in the morning that there's still a chill in the air.

Not quite knowing what to say, I ask if he's had breakfast. He replies that He hasn't. I bring him into my kitchen. I ask him if bacon and eggs would be acceptable. He said that would be fine.

As I'm cooking, I can't seem to stop talking. "Lord, I feel as if you have been ever present at my side. You have been with me through the good times and through the bad, the thick, and the thin. And, Lord, you know how thin some of those times were. But we have been friends for a long time, Lord, and I knew I could place my whole trust in You at those moments. When bad things happen, you don't change what has happened; instead, you send people... people with good, prayerful hearts. And they pray. As Therese of Lisieux, the Little Flower, said, 'Prayer is a surge of the heart.' And I have been on the receiving end of those heart-surges from those good people. Like when I was following my son's casket into church for his funeral Mass. It was the moment I had dreaded the most. But as I walked up the church steps I saw that the church parking lot didn't have any cars parked there. No... the parking lot was filled with hundreds of uniformed police officers standing at attention as the body of one of their fellow police officers, my son's, was carried into church! Lord, I was stunned. I felt as though I was seeing, not people, but their prayers! I actually felt their prayers carrying me. And the same thing happened at the cemetery, where there were thousands of uniformed officers whose prayerful hearts were surging."

"Lord, I know your Spirit remains with us always. I hope this gives You the opportunity to see the world, Your Creation, through our eyes. Lord, we treasure the beauty that surrounds us, winter, spring, summer, and fall. Yes, Lord, sometimes we DO complain about the midsummer heat or having 32" of snow fall in one single winter's day. You know how we are, Lord, some days there's just no pleasing us. But then You open our eyes a little wider and we appreciate those precious blue-sky summer days or the delicacy of the silence during a snowfall. You bring us to a halt so that we can see, really see the beauty of Your Creation. And then, Lord, we are humbled and awestruck. We praise you, Lord, we bless You, we adore You, and we glorify You. Forever, Lord, forever."

"Pancakes tomorrow, Lord?"

Isn't it wonderful having Jesus' presence ~~ no words...
just holy silence. I believe Jesus looks forward to coming.
Back again for those pancakes... and another faithful chat
with Judy.

True faith is given to all who read this!

What did you learn from this sharing?

Michael O'Hara... a faith pilgrim

I would invite Jesus to have breakfast at a cozy Irish pub. We would have all the Irish Breakfast trimmings.

I would have many questions for Jesus: Why am I here? What would you have me do here? What am I getting wrong?

Jesus would look at me with such kindness and say, "Let your faith as small as a mustard seed lead you and let my light of love lessen your worries. All shall pass, the good and the bad. My love will be there forever."

Jesus gives me much to think about. He tells me he will return and take me to have breakfast at the River Jordan and eat fish. This is where Jesus was baptized. I think to myself... Jesus is all about giving life.

It is good to share your questions, ponderings and worries with Jesus... he is a divine listener.

We are created in God's likeness ~~ given free will...
to do what is right.

What did you learn from this sharing?

Barbara Grandi... a courageous woman

I would invite Jesus to my nice apartment. It reminds me of where Jesus was born in Bethlehem. It is not modern or a mansion... I live there simply. Jesus knows he is always welcome at my home.

I would serve Jesus homemade French toast, coffee and some special danish. I would ask Jesus how he is doing and tell him it must be hard to have the whole world talking to him, waiting for answers or miracles and sometimes wanting things that are not always good for them. I am guilty of that also so I turn to my faith and hope for him to show me a better way of thinking and being.

I will also vent to him about my life and problems but he knows them already. Still he is ever so patient and listens deeply. Because of that I feel comfortable pouring my heart out to him and start to feel deep peace. Jesus calms my fears. I felt during this pandemic that he held my hand and calmed my spirits. I have learned to trust Jesus.

If he comes back and invites me for breakfast somewhere alone or with other people I will be ever so happy. Just to be included means so much to me. It is a blessing to share his presence with others.

I won't forget that day when Jesus came to my humble home. He enjoyed his meal and as he was leaving he said, "Barbara, you are special and loved. God doesn't make junk."

Barbara shared how important it is to trust Jesus more. You might just say trusting is the grace to resurrect again and again. We grow strong at the broken places in our life…and then amazingly use these healing places to be for others.

When we pray to Jesus... he is there listening
with his whole heart. You will always be
included in Jesus' love

What did you learn from this sharing?

Fran Catalano... Rosary Society lady from Sacred Heart in Bayside

I would invite Jesus to go to Rome with me and have breakfast with Pope Francis. I would hope he would order whatever he likes. I would suggest eggs and good Italian bread.

We would chat about the world situation and what is the best way to be and act. He leaves me with a blessing and a promise to come again. I just treasure being with him.

... to treasure Jesus' presence is truly a special Faith gift. Imagine just having an "ordinary" chat with Jesus. You can... every day in your humble prayers.

Great choice for a breakfast companion ~~ Pope Francis.
I bet the two of you would pray the rosary
together for world peace.

What did you learn from this sharing?

Father Tom Brosnan... Brooklyn Diocese

I would invite Jesus to Sheepshead Bay, Brooklyn, New York... where the fishing boats might remind him of the Lake Galilee and the old folks walking along the shore might be speaking Brooklynese with a Yiddish tint. The restaurant, by the way, would have to be kosher~~Jesus might not be aware of the revolutionary results of the First Ecumenical Council of Jerusalem!

I would definitely serve him Chilean Sea Bass (though I'd call it Tilapia in an ecologically-sensitive spirit of la Laudato Si) which some would-be archeologists have suggested is what he ate after the resurrection when he prepared breakfast for Peter and the others after their night of fishing. Don't worry, I'd warn him to look out for the coins from Caesar's Casino that sometimes gets lodged in the fishes' mouths when they swim up from Atlantic City! We would talk about the weather for sure. But I'd sneak in a question or two about all the terrible suffering that goes on under his father's watch. Maybe a delicately phrased probe about how he thought the sex abuse scandal happened and was subsequently handled. I would ask him as church ministers how we could be more compassionate.

Believe it or not, something Jesus shared that touched my heart was Jesus' Hypostatic Union... his being two natures in one person. I know that doesn't sound "touching" at all. But I figured if he could be the same person while possessing two distinct natures, I could be grateful for both my birth and adoptive "natures". Thanks to that conviction

I took the scary step (some 35 years ago) to search and find the woman who gave me birth. And just last year, through the wonders of DNA tracing, I found my birth-father's other children. I went from being raised an only child to becoming the eldest of nine siblings. You really can have two sets of parents and a blended family. A "hypostatic" union of sorts, combining nature and nurture, heredity and environment, body and soul ~~ all that while not negating the importance of either inheritance, just like Jesus being completely divine and totally human. I can see him blessing me with wonderful joy at that breakfast.

As Father Tom shared his Good News, bet we all smiled knowing Jesus was with him on his long journey to discover more of family love in his life.

What did you learn from this sharing?

Frank Orlando... a wonderful neighbor called friend

I would invite Jesus to my home that I love so much. I would serve him a plate of pancakes and eggs with good brewed coffee made by my wife JoJo.

I would talk about what he means to me and also how much my family and friends mean to me. I would thank him for what he gave up for us. He knows I thank him in my last prayer of each evening for all his love.

He tells JoJo and me how much he loves us and how much he enjoyed the breakfast JoJo says, "You have to come back again." He tells her, "Next time I will take you and Frank to a big open field of grass, trees and flowers so we can have a big outdoor breakfast and enjoy all of his beauty in the gift of nature."

The two of us are so happy we cannot wait for the next breakfast with Jesus. We stay up all night talking about his special visit to our home ....it was so peaceful. JoJo is already planning the next breakfast menu!

A visit to a home of love…listening hearts hearing Jesus call to love. Frank and JoJo are "heart to heart" with their love of Jesus.

What did you learn from this sharing?

Sister Sally Butler, O.P. ... a "courageous spirit"

I would invite Jesus to Ashland Place in Brooklyn where I lived for over 40 years. Hmmmm... I would serve him a cheese omelet, a Brooklyn bagel and good warm coffee. I would thank him for his support and help on this last tour of duty; grateful for my family and friends and freedom to love God in my own way.

He tells me love is right where I am. I tell him I loved the opera, watching the little children in the day programs and the green gardens we planted amidst the concrete of city life.

When he comes again I say Lord...lets go to Ireland. He says I knew you would take me to Ireland. We both smile as we land on the green soil of my ancestors.

90 years of living life... knowing the Lord is there in the cement and concrete in life. Believe... love is everywhere our spirit is. Sister Sally, you have a great Brooklyn heart and spirit of Faith.

What did you learn from this sharing?

Sister Corita Ryan, O.P. ... one "good listener"

I never thought of this... but I do believe I would invite Jesus to Eucharist at mass. I would serve Jesus my love. I don't chat a lot but I am a good listener. I would love to listen to all he has to say to me. I listen in the silence of my heart and hear the Lord say to me... "take and eat".

The next time Jesus comes because he is so thoughtful, I think he would invite me downstairs to our beautiful chapel because he knows that's where we meet as often as we can. He tries to make it easy on me and all of us due to the restrictions placed on us due to COVID.

Being a "good listener" is a gift. It enables one to truly hear, believe and understand what is being said. To be a listener is a blessing.

What did you learn from this sharing?

Paige Accardi... age 11

I would invite Jesus to my house and make him my favorites~~cereal, waffles and cinnamon toast. First, I would show him my room and all my stuff. I would ask him about what heaven was like. I would ask him if he knew my Poppy?

He tells me that heaven is a happy and peaceful place where everyone gets along. Yes, he tells me that he knows my Poppy and that everyone likes him and his stories.
If he came to earth again, I think he would take me to an old-fashioned diner in Bethlehem where he was born.

He would tell me to be my best self, keep my chin up and always persevere through hard times. To have a good mindset by setting my intentions on good outcomes; and to pray about everything.

Young people sure know how to have a good conversation with Jesus.

What did you learn from this sharing?

Mia (age 12) and Claire (age 8)... Paige Accardi's sisters

Mia would take Jesus to Williston Park Diner (her favorite). **Claire** would take him to Shake Shack in case he never had a shake.

Mia would ask him if heaven was bright with golden roads and gates. **Claire** asked him what he did in heaven... did he have a job? Jesus told them he takes care of people.

When he comes back again to visit earth **Mia** said he would take her to Panera her other favorite place to eat. **Claire** would go with Jesus to Wendy's.

Jesus would tell Claire to live every moment well and laugh every day. Don't let anyone get in the way of your happiness. Include everyone when playing, be kind and make others laugh when they are sad. He tells the sisters... Paige, Mia and Claire that he loves them and will be their friend forever. The three sisters hug each other as Jesus blesses them.

Let the little children lead us... to the heart of Jesus.

What did you learn from this sharing?

Kathy Accardi... a loving grandmother

I would invite Jesus into my home where he is always welcome. I would serve him my family's favorite... homemade banana bread and overnight French toast.

We would chat about how he enjoys when I talk to him and ask for his guidance. We would chat about what the future would bring. He would tell me never to forget that he loves me and that I was created to be me and not worry about being accepted or pleasing others.

He knows that I love him and want to follow his example and he knows that I am weak and human and ready to forgive me.

I love surprises so I will let him surprise me and take me where he wants when he comes to earth again. I know it will be amazing. Jesus asks me to keep striving to be my best, to believe in myself, to believe that I am worthy of his love and to include him in every detail of my life. Not to worry about my children... he has them under his wings. He tells me as he blesses me to keep expressing my gratefulness and praise by the way I live my life.

Jesus speaks to our hearts...let's do the same. Wonderful to look forward to his coming again to breakfast...especially at a surprise place. Where would that be for you?

What did you learn from this sharing?

Florence Clark... related by being a friend

I invite Jesus to the table I eat my meals at. I serve him juice and then would offer him a breakfast menu of eggs, French toast and whatever else he would like to eat.

This made me think of all the choices we have to make in life... some that we can control and others that we are led to make. For example, in grade school I wanted to go to Bishop McDonald High School but didn't get picked so I went to Our Lady of Wisdom Academy. I now feel Jesus led me to where I belonged. I still have friends from there and the good sisters pushed us to be all that we could... those sisters were way ahead of their time!

Life seems to always be filled with choices... some easy... some not so easy. However, I do think Jesus gently guides us. The trick is to learn to listen to him. I certainly am happy to be with Jesus today. So happy He came to visit.

When Jesus invites me to breakfast I hope it will be under a tree. I listened to a sermon about a tree and its' branches. I am one of those branches blessed by Jesus love. Jesus reminds me that there are different types of trees. Oaks are strong to lift people up who have fallen. Willows are waning and usually grow by water to refresh people who are hungry. Maybe for God's comfort Elms give off shade on a hot day. Some people who are worn out by the heat of hard work or hard times or had trying conditions in their lives could find relief under the shade of the Elm that could represent Jesus' love.

I am happy I can chat with Jesus… He tells me I am a loving branch. Jesus blesses me and promises to come back again. He smiles gently as He points to a tree in my yard.

Florence and Jesus have a good conversation about choices in life… the tree and the branches metaphor are so life-giving

What did you learn from this sharing?

Mrs. Frances Rhymes... holy lady from Saturday Phone Prayer Chat

My husband Clyde is a wonderful chef so I will invite Jesus to my home and Clyde will prepare a wonderful home cooked meal with lots of wine!

Our conversation will first be full of gratitude for all the blessings his Father bestowed upon me and my 89 years of life. Then I would share my concern about the darkness in life that is trying to gain control over humanity.

I am concerned that his Father is sending us a message with COVID, the fires, droughts and man's inhumanity to man and animals. I will ask for the Lord's direction in how I can share His love.

The Lord tells me to keep praying... and stay on that wonderful Saturday Prayer Chat.

Mrs. Rhymes has lots of Faith. Her sharing that we humans need to be more caring with each other and our environment is exactly what Jesus asks of us.

What did you learn from this sharing?

"Heavenly" Tender Peach Scones.

Submitted by Sister Ave, O.P.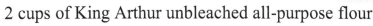

Preheat oven to 375 degrees

Mix dry ingredients:

2 cups of King Arthur unbleached all-purpose flour

½ teaspoon salt

1/3 cup sugar

optional   ¼ teaspoon of nutmeg or cinnamon spice

1 tablespoon baking soda

Whisk together thoroughly

Cut 6 tablespoons of unsalted butter into small cubes

With fork mix into dry ingredients

Add 2 large eggs

1/3 cup plain yogurt or sour cream

½ teaspoon of almond extract

Combine all ingredients…whisk together gently

Now fold into batter 1 cup of "heavenly" fresh diced
    peaches... batter will be sticky

Drop onto baking sheet like a drop cookie or use scone pan

Bake for 20-25 minutes until a golden brown

Serve warm plain, or with butter or warm jam…

have an extra bowl of cut peaches next to plate of

"heavenly" scones.

Save time

Order a box of Peaches and Cream Scone mix from King Arthur.
Mix and bake…delicious!

"... a recipe is a story that ends with a good meal."
(Pat Conroy)

Arlene Moss... devoted member of prayer groups

Lord Jesus, enter into my home, the Home that you built (Psalm 127:1) and have provided for me. Here, please eat and enjoy this fresh baked loaf of bread and cup of wine for the communion of our souls. The simpler fare... just as you served your disciples.

The conversation, Lord, is seasoned with thanksgivings for all your benefits that have been available to me through the cross. I hear your beautiful audible voice confirming all the gifts of heaven you so willingly and graciously bestow on all who believe.

I hear you saying how much, how very much you love me and all humanity. So much, such unconditional love flowing directly from your Father's heart. Through your heart to me and all who believe and receive, even those who do not... yet.

Because You are the same yesterday, today and tomorrow your words of conversation remain the same... always full of love. No amount of foreknowledge can compare to the Presence of Your Love.

You rise from my table, extend your hand and say, "Come, I invite you to share the breakfast I prepare for you." In an instant we are on the seashore, a fire is roasting a fresh fish, cleaned, pure and salted ~~perfect in its preparation. In the simplicity of this meal there is a feeling of heavenly splendor.

And Lord, you say to me, "Come, eat this gift as it is the fullness of of forgiveness, redemption and restoration. You believe in me... I ask that you continue to believe in me. As you consume this meal may the truth in you be radiated to all whom I send into your path. I ask, I have always asked, I continue to ask... and only believe."
(John 6:29) I know the Lord will return as he always does...

As you read and reflected on Arlene's sharing I am sure you felt drawn into her prayer of loving Jesus. What is your prayer?

What did you learn from this sharing?

Angela Lewis… a trusting heart

I invite Jesus to breakfast with me at sunrise on a beach. I am not really a breakfast person, but I will offer Jesus a bagel with cream cheese and lox and an ice coffee latte. He smiles at me.

I begin our conversation by extending gratitude for all the graces he has given to me. I ask him to help me process the challenges I face, assistance on how to forgive and the wisdom to share the abundance of love He gives to me.

Jesus shows me what it means to love my neighbor as myself even those who have caused me harm. I ask Jesus to remind me of His presence in my life and to help me to live a life that honors him.

Jesus surprises me and says "lets meet here tomorrow and invite a few people." I will invite my mom for her strength to family and to her faith. I also invite my loving husband Rey for his dedication to all of his endeavors from business to faith. I invite two good friends… Father Gordon and Sister Ave for all that they are and all that they do for the people of God.

I look forward to being at the sunrise on the beach with the Lord. After I was hit by a train many years ago, one of the persons who came to visit me in the hospital was Angela. Perhaps when we share our caring for one another, that is the sunrise of God's love.

What did you learn from this sharing?

Mount Saint Dominic Academy, my high school alma mater in Caldwell, New Jersey

I asked the May 2021 Freshman Religion Class a few questions about having Breakfast with Jesus. Their answers follow.

Where would you invite Jesus for breakfast?
Waffle House
Diner
Beach
Pancake House
At my house
Picnic at a park at sunrise

What would you serve him?
home-made waffles
pancakes
avocado toast
fruit salad
bagels (best breakfast food in New Jersey)

What would you talk about with Jesus?
advice for the future
best way to be happy
how are relatives in heaven doing
do pets go to heaven
friends
am I living the life I should

thoughts about sports

does it hurt to die

can he tell us the future

What is something Jesus shares that touches your heart.

tells us about loved ones in heaven

tells a fun fact about a family member that makes you smile

says he enjoys the meal with you and not just the syrup on waffles and pancakes

When he comes again, where does he invite you for breakfast?

beach where it is peaceful, quiet and beautiful

Jerusalem

a mountain

somewhere peaceful and calm untouched by society

where people less fortunate live

heaven

at a campfire

These young women definitely could picture having breakfast with Jesus. Their thoughts are so honest and sincere. You get a sense from their sharings that they know and believe in Jesus' presence in their lives.

Go back and re-read their answers to the questions where Jesus would invite them for breakfast on his return visit to earth.

My sister, Ave, went to Mount Saint Dominic Academy.
She loved that high school. I wonder what
Jesus thought of how you all turned out...
pretty impressed I guess.

What did you learn from this sharing?

Sister Diane Capuano, O.P. ... sings and plays guitar at community gatherings

I was just so thrilled of thinking of Jesus coming for breakfast. I would serve him a simple breakfast in my living room. We sit in comfortable chairs. I serve him my heart, soul and mind.

Jesus is so easy to be with. We chat of anything and everything. It is such a grace for the two of us to be spending quality time together. What was truly a blessing was that there did not need to be much chatter. I just enjoyed the beautiful, sacred silence of His holy presence.

I know Jesus is always present and quite often I just sense Jesus deeply within me and that relaxes me. Jesus tells me He will come for another visit to this same place. He tells me He enjoyed each and every moment in the lovely home and sitting in my comfortable blue chair. We both say thank you at the same time.

This visit with Jesus sounded so peaceful, quiet and full of harmony. I wonder if Sister Diane sang for Jesus...if she did... the Lord was delighted.

"Silence is golden"!

What did you learn from this sharing?

Jane Liello... a heart to heart friend from Kentucky

I would invite Jesus for breakfast at the Sea of Galilee where He instructed His disciples to cast out their fishing nets. After a night without catching any fish, they "trusted". I too, want to be more trusting in life.

Then I thought if Jesus came to my home, I would serve Him some eggs, bacon and fresh juice and some of my husband John's homemade bread with good hot coffee. John would cut him a big piece of bread and break it for him. Jesus would bless the meal.

I would tell Jesus how much my faith has grown over the years. One example was how I prayed our grandchildren's adoption would be finalized. I prayed for a long time and felt God would answer my prayers. He did. Now I can thank him in person.

Jesus touches my heart when he says, "come to me all you who labor and I will give your rest". To me labor can be more than physical work. My heart and my mind can "labor" with hurts done to me, hurts I may have done to others, worries and not listening to God. Not holding grudges, looking at the part I played, and saying sincerely that I am sorry is pleasing to God. Jesus listens and nods compassion at me as I share.

Jesus tells me He will come again for breakfast and take me to the Basilica of the Annunciation. He says this is where the angel announced to Mary that she would be the Mother of God. He says, "Jane, all things are possible when one trusts and believes that they are not alone". I can't wait for that wonderful visit.

We can see from Jane's sharing that prayer is truly a gift of God's grace. Our everyday Yes to God brings great comfort, peace and joy for sure. May the blessing of the five loaves and two fish be your blessing every day.

What did you learn from this sharing?

Adam Morris... a friend from Missouri

I would invite Jesus off a windy mountain road on the island of Maui, there's a small side road that goes down to a small village. And in this village, there's a little shack that serves the best banana bread in the world, Aunt Sadie's. I'd ask Jesus to meet me there.

I would give him a few pieces of Aunt Sadie's banana bread, fresh out of the oven. I would also pour him a good hot cup of coffee. We would walk the road into the village, with the sea on one side and a little country church on the other side.

I would tell him that my wife and I came here on our twentieth anniversary and would love to live here someday. It is so peaceful. Jesus nods. I would then tell Him of my worries about our country, that it feels like we're headed for another civil war... even the church is divided. Jesus listens.

He reminds me of free will and that faith is personal and that everyone treats their faith differently. And that people publicly using their faith are in the minority and that most people in America, Christian or not, share my worries, that though we may disagree on specifics, we have more in common than not. That sure made me feel better. He tells me to trust God for it to work out the way it is meant to.

We went to the little church and sat quietly for a few minutes and then headed out to the ocean, waves breaking on the rough volcanic rocks on the shore. He reminds me that it is getting late and I had a long trip ahead of me. I asked where he was going now. He said not to worry and that he had his own way home... now I smile! I leave the village, making my way back to the car, to the airport and ordinary America.

Sometime later I get a letter from Jesus with directions to a small town in Israel. A little nervous I make my preparations and go there. We sit in a small café on the shore of a large, calm lake sipping good coffee and eating something made of sweet dough and nuts. He asks me about my trip. I tell him what I saw... the large military presence, the checkpoints, the sense of tense urgency. He points out to me that this is a country at war, and has been for a very long time. And yet, He reminds me that life continues. People have families, build community, eat, pray, live and love. Troubled times will come and go and no matter how difficult it gets there will always be those who have it better and those who have it worse. Jesus then says, "Find the good, share the love and pass it on. You may just find that good and love returned to you in time." I think Jesus is showing me a better way to live and be for others.

Then he takes me down to the lake, and He speaks to the fishermen (and one or two fisherwomen) and He tells me this is how things endure. They were fishing on this lake in these boats, when I was last her... he winks. We get in one of the boats and spend the day with the fishermen, catching fish and sharing a few laughs... mostly
about my lack of skill at fishing. When we return at the day's end, tired and hungry, I hear thunder in the distance.

The fisherfolk frown and pack up their things to head home.

I look at Jesus who reminds me that this is another way in which the world endures... despite the thunder people go to work, provide for their families and go home to spend time with them. "Even", he says solemnly, "when the thunder isn't from the lighting in the skies, but from fighting here on earth". Then he says, "Go in peace and share it everywhere you go."

Perhaps Jesus did answer Adam's thoughts about the world... that each one of us makes choices to create life-giving spaces for one another. Think about that!

What did you learn from this sharing?

Adolfo Quezada... spiritual writer and friend from Arizona

I would invite Jesus to breakfast in my home or perhaps to the restaurant of his choice. I would serve him salmon or I would ask him what he would prefer eating. I would let him know how wonderful it was to be in His presence; then, I would just listen to what he had to say to me.

Hmm... We might even stop by the library for some bagels and cream cheese. There we could discuss a future book I hope to write. Jesus says, "Keep sharing your spiritual insights."

Jesus stays with me not just for breakfast but the whole day. On the way home, I take him to the pancake house. I show him the menu with a variety of pancakes. He says, "Let's share an order". I smile and know Jesus is showing me that "enough is enough" and don't waste food. He smiles as he pours blueberry syrup on his two pancakes. "I think I will try that syrup today". He winks!

Jesus says next time I will take you to the biggest Barnes and Nobles store and hands me a gift certificate for a holy book. I so enjoyed my day with him and cannot wait for another day with my Lord.

Adolfo shows us the gift of having a friend like Jesus in our life and also how Christ shares his life with us unconditionally.

Pancakes are the favorite! Bet Jesus is smiling!
His presence is an <u>extra</u> <u>blessing</u>
early in the morning.

What did you learn from this sharing?

Thelma l. Greaves-Hawkins... a compassionate heart

I would invite Jesus for breakfast at my favorite place... the Cayman Islands. The breakfast menu would be bacon, sausage, eggs and pancakes and/or homemade biscuits, tea, coffee and orange juice. Yum!

The first thing I would say to Jesus is thank you for being number one in my life. Thank you for always being there and listening to me.

I would ask him why there is so much hate in the world. I know there is plenty of love and the hatred might be miniscule but what we see and hear is devastating. The hatred against people of color, the atrocious treatment of some people in parts of the world is unforgivable. I would ask him how we can help him to cure this madness. Being with Jesus gives me a feeling of tremendous joy. A feeling of wanting to sing and dance.

The next time Jesus comes, he takes us to Ghana the home of one of his priests. I would invite my husband because of his great caring of his fellow man. I would invite my daughter Cheryl... she loves twitter. She brings humor to all political conversations. Everything is hilarious with her. I would also bring my daughter Angela because of her tremendous love of Jesus and her quiet demeanor in sharing the Lord's word and bringing people closer to Him. Last but not least I would bring my youngest daughter, Vanessa, who is the biggest conspiracy theorist in a young person that I have ever experienced. I would enjoy hearing her conversation with Jesus   I would just be so happy my family could have this special time with Jesus.

Something tells me Jesus would have a wonderful time with Thelma and her family. Jesus loves when we share ourselves in honest and open ways.

What did you learn from this sharing?

Helen Quigley... Third Order Carmelite

I would like to invite Jesus into the home of my heart. First, I would wash his feet as a sign of hospitality. Then I would serve him tea with lemon and honey, Irish soda bread and fresh salmon (I know He likes fish!)

Jesus and I would chat about my life and I ask him if he thought I followed his will. He smiles at me and says, "You sure have." Jesus thanked me for caring for those in need by providing hospice care at Calvary Hospital. He says, "I love you with an everlasting love."

The next time Jesus comes he will invite me to the waterfront in Beacon, New York. It was there at a retreat that I felt his presence in my life. During the retreat I went to a quiet place and wrote a letter to my dear deceased mother. I sat crying with grief. As I looked up from my writing pad the river was sparkling with sunlight... I felt Jesus was answering me. I still have that letter after 29 years. It still brings comfort to my tears.

Helen's visit with Jesus is full of comfort and peace. This is something we all need at some time in our life.

Her home is her castle...very humble.

What did you learn from this sharing?

Nina Siggia... a friend from Brooklyn

I would invite Jesus to the Canarsie Pier in Brooklyn on a bright, sunny day under the shade of a huge tree. There is a cool breeze blowing off the Jamaica Bay. This is such a peaceful place to take Jesus.

I bring a nice breakfast of coffee, juice, bagels and cold cereal (cheerios!) I see he takes a big bowl of cheerios and gives me a smile. We eat and pray together. As we enjoy each other's company we talk freely about many topics.

Jesus looks right into my heart and says, "Do not fret! Be at peace and do not be afraid, I am always with you... you are loved." Jesus knows that I love him also as I say that every day in my morning and evening prayers. As Jesus departs I feel tears welling up in my eyes. He says, "Nina, I will come again to visit. Bring cheerios again!" He blesses me and my tears disappear.

Nina shared her faithful heart with the Lord... something we all need to do. "Heart" shaped Cherrios, I hope!

What did you learn from this sharing?

193

Father Thomas Ahern... Good Pastor in Brooklyn, NY

I would invite him to come to the rectory kitchen for breakfast. I would imagine it will be a full table with the retired priests ready to share some holy stories. I would serve him and everyone at the table fruits, toast and eggs sunny side up.

We would chat of eternal life and heaven and how the good we do here on earth for others helps us to get there. Jesus would tell us to do all in his name.

He tells us he will come again and take us all to the Sea of Galilee and he would serve us fish there. We all give him a round of applause. Then he tells us to be courageous... and break bread by sharing compassion and hope with all those we serve. We all say Amen.

Well, that is Father Ahern...he shared Jesus and breakfast with the retired priest friends who live with him. Maybe Jesus gave a round of applause as he left the rectory looking back as Father Ahern waved at him from the porch.

What did you learn from this sharing?

Sister Maureen Chase, O.P. ... Pastoral Minister Chaplain, Nassau University Medical Center

I would invite Jesus to share breakfast with me on the patio in my backyard, especially during the Spring, Summer or Fall seasons. It is a quiet and serene sanctuary with many different species of birds and a family of bunnies who have made it their home. Each year in the Spring, a pair of Mourning Doves inhabit the hanging basket as their "birthing" room. To watch them give birth, nurture, teach and feed their young is an incredible experience of "new-life" faithfulness and amazing parenting. Because this wonder of creation has been such a gift to me, I would like to share this experience and my gratitude with Jesus.

We would probably enjoy a simple breakfast of cinnamon bagels and tea. We would talk about the ups and downs of life with its joys and challenges. I would probably ask many questions, especially regarding the pediatric patients and families whom I have journeyed with through their sufferings of cancer and AIDS. I would also thank Jesus for his unconditional love and presence in my life and for the gifts I have received, including the Mourning Doves. I'm sure I would be touched by the feelings Jesus might share with me regarding his acceptance, understanding, frustrations, unconditional love and gifts of grace given to each of us as he walks with us in the highs and lows of our lives.

Jesus would probably ask me where I would like to share breakfast with him when he returns for another visit. I would most likely suggest the same place... back to my patio, a simple and peace-filled place to have our breakfast sharing.

You could certainly feel the peace on Sister Maureen's patio and how she and Jesus smiled at those "Mourning Doves" reminding us that every day brings new life and our faith-filled responses. Their conversation was so heart to heart. You could sense Jesus' affirmations of grace for Sister Maureen in her hospital ministry of being his love for others. Jesus will definitely come back for a patio breakfast of simplicity and peace.

What did you learn from this sharing?

Patty and Dan Callahan... Long Island friends

We would take Jesus to our favorite "bagel" place and perhaps he might like to try their lox and bagels. Humm... maybe we might suggest pancakes too (Dan's favorite breakfast).

(Dan) I would talk to him about dandelions and ragweed that I've been concerned about this season. I'd ask for divine intervention and I see him giving me a divine grin. I would also share with him my grief for my brother and sister who died this year and my good friend Manny who passed a few months ago. And also, how this one high school buddy of mine that is still here who is so aggravating. Jesus looks at me with such compassion for all I have shared. I think he will come again and take the two of us to the Golden Rod in York Beach, Maine because it's very special and meaningful to me and my siblings... the Goldendrod and Nubble Lighthouse. I cry just thinking about those two places and their connection with my family growing up. Jesus would be happy to help me re-connect with my brothers and sisters on a deeper level. He shows me that memories are good to have and help us to heal our grief.

(Patty) I would ask the Lord to watch over all my family members and draw them closer to your heart of love. We'd go to Coney Island with Jesus and buy Him a knish and hot dog. He'd take me on the roller coaster ride. I'd be scared but with Jesus with me I know my fear would lessen and I would have lots of fun. I didn't have lots of fun growing up. I had too much responsibility. Jesus would say, "I have come to give you life. Have a fun day today". I sure would with my dear husband Dan and Jesus right by my side.

Jesus speaks to our hearts… He says, "put your loved one in my hands and trust". Then he would add… "fear not, I understand your grief and know the pain of separation". I am right there with you in that feeling of loss and sadness. Now, as far as the ragweed and dandelions go, we'll figure that out together with Freddy the Landscaper.

Even as adults we need comfort… Jesus is there for us. Even as adults we need happy days… Jesus is there for us.

Hmmm… those weeds. Sometimes out of something you think is bad, something good can grow.

What did you learn from this sharing?

Father Bob Lauder... author of many fine spiritual books

I would invite Jesus to the dining room for senior priests in Douglaston, New York. I wonder what he would think of all of us. He smiles an engaging smile with all.

I notice he goes from table to table. He blesses all of us. I bring Jesus a plate of warm sausages and eggs... what I love to eat. He picks up his fork and smiles. So do I!

He chats with us about the contemporary church and says all priests no matter what their age reflect Christ's love to others. He listens to each one of us. He says, "Wherever you are", (he points to the sign for senior priests) "Christ is right here". We all applaud him.

Jesus is comfortable just being himself as he brings his empty plate to the kitchen to thank the kitchen workers. He says he will come back again to visit all of us. I think later about the visit and his message. Right here... Christ lives in you... in me.

Father Lauder had an interesting visit with Jesus...and he believes what Jesus said...right where you are Christ reveals his love. Think about that!

Knowing Jesus is a forgiving God helps to open our heart to him. Jesus teaches us to be grateful.

What did you learn from this sharing?

Beef Wellington – A Labor of Love

 Short story ... this Beef Wellington dish is my signature dish to make. Yes, and I have made it only twice. On February 14, 2019 I made it for Valentine's Day Dinner with six guests (including Peggy and myself) Bruce and Carol Meyers and Mitch and Kathy Cobert. These two couples are special, so as the "ole saying goes", **I put the dog on everything was "top drawer".** From appetizers to cocktails to the "Dinner" and dessert and expresso. The compliments were wonderful, clearing the plates from the table was funny, they were licked clean. I think anyone can prepare this recipe. I followed Gordon Ramsey on his you tube each time and all turned out well. I will give you the ingredients but you should watch the Gordon Ramsey Beef Wellington video on how to put it all together. He makes it fun and easy. And you will find out it is a "**Labor of Love**" to do.

Ingredients for Beef Wellington:

serving of beef (filet) for 6 people

two large boxes of wild mushrooms (remove stems) or buy with stems.

olive oil 2 tbs.

puff pastry dough 2 boxes

Thyme 1 sprig (don't use stem

Parma Ham 10 slices

2 egg yolks beaten with 1 tbs. water

pinch of sea salt and pepper

Red wine sauce

2 tbs. olive oil

beef trimmings (I get a one-pound package of good filet beef cut up)

4 large shallots peeled and cut up

12 peppercorns

1 bay leaf

1 thyme sprig (don't use stem)

splash of red wine vinegar

1 750 ml red wine (yes use the whole bottle)

750 ml beef stock

You believe this! Well like I said watch, the video first a couple of times (**Labor of Love**). The more you watch the video the more you want to make it. I watch this video as I prepare it. Get organized in the kitchen, prepare the site you'll be working in. I found total prep time was under an hour. For me to explain mixture and prep would be ten pages when it's really cut and dry from Gordon Ramsey. It is truly my "**Labor of Love**". Bon Appetit!

Submitted by Joe Clark

"...if there is a recipe for goodness in life~~ it starts with picking the very best of ingredients"

Christ the King and Queen of Martyrs Students 2021 Confirmation Retreat

Where would you invite Jesus for breakfast?
IHop
a garden
to my house
to a park and anywhere that is peaceful
to my church
my apartment
to a café with an outside table
to a field on a hillside
on top of Bear Mountain
to the forest
to my grandma's home

What would you serve him?
hash brown and pancakes
fruit salad with eggs and bread
bread and wine
French toast
a pop-tart
some fish
ordinary breakfast with some waffles
my grandma's arepas
a nice big nutritious meal
tea and breakfast cakes
western omelet

my favorite food… pasta
a well-cooked warm meal

What would you chat about?
what should I do to bond with God
about Confirmation and the spirit coming into my life
his plans for me and how I can carry them out
I would chat about heaven
about the issues going on in my life and ask for
strength/help
my family
how to share love and caring openly
school
advice, questions, wonderings

What would he tell you?
give reassurances
tell me to love myself and others with respect
you need self-love in a good way
to be good to my mom
follow my dreams
accepts me as I am
be brave
he is always with me especially when I am afraid
about the pets in heaven
keep the faith
that he is proud of me and needs me to serve
that to have hope and never give up

What does he ask of you?

to spread his gospel
to create a good future for all people
be God's peace everywhere you go
help others to keep the faith
to always pray
to be respectful
to be happy
to listen to my parents
what I am doing with my life
to be a joyful person

Isn't it wonderful how these young people were so happy to have Jesus come for breakfast and prepare a delicious meal. I feel these students really listen to the word of God and strive to live it well.

All these young people giving a sharing back
to Jesus are examples to me
of being "faithful".

What did you learn from this sharing?

Paula Santoro... nurse and social worker

I would invite Jesus to my daughter's home to meet Donna and her husband and my new grandson. I think they would be thrilled to meet Jesus in person.

What I would serve would be up to Donna, who is an incredible cook. I know it would be something nourishing. Jesus would bless their little family.

I would talk about the state of the world right now and ask Jesus as individuals what could we each do to make things better for everyone. Jesus would remind each one of us that we are called to be peace-givers.

The next time Jesus comes for breakfast would be at my home. There Jesus will meet my son Chuck who would prepare quite a delicious breakfast for Jesus. Both my children are better cooks than me! I think Chuck and Jesus would have a great conversation. He blesses us again as he leaves. I feel so happy to have Jesus meet my wonderful children that I love so much.

Jesus understands family life… he enjoys meeting family members just where they are. He knows how much parents love their children (adult children, too!). Paula has a great spirit and a loving heart.

What did you learn from this sharing?

Laura Cerami... retreatant at Tabor in Oceanside, NY

I would invite Jesus to my home. We would sit on the nice deck. I would serve him fresh fruit and some pancakes. I would be so thrilled to be in the Lord's company.

There would be wisdom sharing and in depth sharing about my life, relationships and my journey of peace.
The Lord would remind me to follow in his footsteps...

...to be loving

...to be trusting

...to care about others.

I look forward to when He returns for another visit. I ponder in my heart what He shared with me.

Pondering, remembering and cherishing a wonderful visit is a grace.

What did you learn from this sharing?

Sister Peg Murphy, O.P. ... a praying heart

I would invite Jesus to breakfast in a secluded garden filled with wild flowers and birds singing under a shaded tree. I would serve Jesus muffins with jam, tea and with an assortment of delicious fresh berries.

I would chat about the extraordinary beauty of nature, the love of the Trinity that gives me peace, love and joy. I would also share how fragile our world is...I know Jesus would be concerned about my thoughts.

He tells me that I am blest and fortunate.... that to whom much is given much is expected. He tells me to pray more for those people who are not as fortunate and to continue to spread kindness and joy.

Next time he comes, Jesus takes me to somewhere in the Mid-East, a place inhabited by persons who are homeless, hungry and tortured. Jesus wants me to share my love and my prayers and sacrifices so that these people also feel loved.

We are so blessed in this country (USA). However, there are people who suffer from poverty, oppression, war and violence. Our prayers and extending our compassion can help people to feel loved.

I think from Sister Peg's sharing we can see how Jesus opens our heart to "be" for one another in our actions and in our prayers.

What did you learn from this sharing?

Kevin Holmes... a mighty fine poet

I would invite Jesus to sit at our family table made of old oak. I would serve him eggs any way he would like. Jesus would smile as I don my kitchen apron. We sit at the table with our hearts opened. We share about family, love, questions, finances a little and future plan.

I stand to do the dishes but feeling different...Feeding the Lamb of God. Arlene, my wife, floats in some thoughts of her own... looks at me and I wink and nod. I make more coffee. The talks are long... stretching out like they do. We are a house of many tongues.

Jesus stands and folds His hands and with full and gentle eyes he says "peace". We nod and wink and know all of us listened with heart peace. We know he will come back again to the old oak table.

Something about that kitchen table that invites heart sharings. Jesus loves to sit at the table of love with us.

A lot of things are shared around an old oak table...
one is to put "peace" into our daily lives

What did you learn from this sharing?

Sister Shamus Eileen Dwyer, O.P. ... a little bit of "Irish" heaven here on earth

I would invite Jesus to my room. I would serve him anything he wishes. We would chat about how best to deal with difficulties especially during this pandemic. I would find Jesus' sharing with me very sensitive and hopeful. He knows I have a great sense of humor so we laugh a lot together. The next time he comes I would like to go where there is water... a place I find so very peaceful. Jesus says, "How about Galilee?"

A sense of humor is healing, affirming and so very joyful. Sister Shamus has shared her joy everyday of her life. She is God's ripple effect of happiness in the world.

> What did you learn from this sharing?

Sister Mary Claire Rhatigan, O.P. ...
plays a ukulele

I would invite Jesus to the beach for breakfast. In fact, I live right across the street from the beach in Long Beach, New York. I would serve him bacon, eggs, cheese on a roll (easy to eat), orange juice, coffee and of course Irish Soda Bread. I think he knows how much I love that bread.

We would chat about the Beauties of Nature and how grateful I felt for my family and friends. I would also share with him my concerns about the problems in the church today. Jesus listens with great compassion.

He thanks me for bringing him to the beach... his favorite place. He tells me that he is always with me and he is right there within the church calling forth new life.

I tell him the next time that we will meet for breakfast at the Cliffs of Moher in County Clare, Ireland. It is the homeland of my ancestors, but not just mine. All my family and friends will be there for a fun reunion including a sing-a-long. Jesus smiles and says he will be there and hopes I will bring my ukulele and sing the good songs I wrote. He makes me so happy.

You sure can feel the enjoyment that this visit was with Jesus and Sister Mary Claire O.P. Imagine that reunion and Jesus singing his heart out with that Irish family.

Jesus is right there in church life giving us his "necessary graces".

What did you learn from this sharing?

Cynthia Alfonso… Astoria friend

I would invite Jesus to a Tropical Island with Palm trees tropical birds, flowers and animals, fruits and fish surrounded by the beautiful ocean. I would thank him for creating this place of beauty.

I would serve him my favorite breakfast: eggs benedict, with fruit, juice and coffee. I would decorate the table we would eat at.

Since I am worried about the future of our country, I would discuss why a country so rich with opportunity is being diminished by negativity. The United States is not perfect… until recently I could not imagine living anywhere else.

Jesus would tell me, "fear not and to pray for peace every day." He would also tell me that greed is not good for a nation, we must learn to be better… Jesus feels we can. This gives me hope.

I think the next time Jesus comes he would take me to the Garden of Eden. There I would see the beauty, peace and tranquility that God intended for us. If we all pray and share forgiveness we could have an earth with peace and harmony among all people.

It is good we can share our concerns with Jesus... he shows us how to live a better way and it is possible. Knowing Jesus wants us to have peace, encourages us to be peace-givers.

> What did you learn from this sharing?

Sister Peggy Byrne, O.P. ... a "joy-filled" Dominican

I would invite Jesus to McDonald's. We would have an Egg McMuffin. I could see the Lord was enjoying it. Me too!

We would talk about the variety of foods on the menu. Then I would tell him about all the people I love... even those in heaven. I would thank the Lord for sending these wonderful people into my life.

I would listen to Jesus and be touched by his caring and telling me that everything will work out especially when I believe. This makes me feel so peaceful.

Jesus says he will return again. I say, "Lord, let's go to a diner, no fancy place". I just am so happy to be with Him. He blesses me and says, "See you soon Sister Peggy at the diner." I am still smiling from His visit.

Jesus and Sister Peggy just like a simple meal and being present to each other. Think of what makes you smile in life. I bet you thank Jesus for that joy.

What did you learn from this sharing?

Mrs. T. Vitalis... a heart friend from Brooklyn

I would invite Jesus to a quiet place where we could listen to each other. I would notice He has a beautiful smile. Then He says…"so do you". This makes me feel so relaxed.

I would serve Jesus bread, ham and some wine. As he blesses it…I bow my head in prayer.

We chat about what will happen tomorrow. I tell him I love him with my whole heart and depend on him to show me and my children the way. He tells me that he will always look over me and keep me safe.

He smiles again… he says he will come back again and find another quiet place where we could continue our sharing.

I can imagine how wonderful the sharing Mrs. Vitalis and Jesus had… choosing a quiet place to feel the presence and peace of the Lord is truly a wonderful way to start the day.

What did you learn from this sharing?

Sister Ave Clark, O.P. ... Heart to Heart Ministry

I would invite Jesus to Denville, New Jersey for brunch at my brother Joe and wife Peggy's home... there is always a welcome mat out there. We would have breakfast on their deck with Jesus. Peggy would cut some of their backyard sunflowers and put them in a vase. Jesus smiles... he says, "Joe, what is that delicious smell." Joe laughs and says, "You know Lord, my specialty of eggs, bacon, sausages and warm bagels."

We talk about their children and grandchildren. (Jesus knows I love being a "great" aunt). Jesus says, "I watch over them every day." All three of us at the same time say, "Thank you Lord." Just before he leaves, Jesus says, "You are my beloved friends" and blesses us. We all have a big Clark "grin" on our faces. Next time Jesus says my treat... and Joe says, "Where is that Lord?" "At your sister "O.P" house in Bayside... she makes delicious peach scones!" After Jesus leaves we all agree... "were not our hearts on fire with love with the Lord here." I look down and see that Jesus left us a note on the patio table that says, "I will always be with you." We hug each other with great joy.

The sunflowers on the table turn toward the sun... we all look up and feel the presence of Jesus still with us. I listen as Joe says, "Boy he sure was easy to talk to." Peggy shares how she could tell Jesus loved their backyard. I feel that Jesus loved our family-oriented chatting and how we all said grace together.

227

I always feel Jesus is smiling at our family gatherings. He gives us the gift of joy to share. Sunflowers remind me of God's deep and steadfast love for each one of us.

Next time, Jesus, at Ave's home you will have
my Beef Wellington ~~ and my sister
will share her "heart-grace".

What did you learn from this sharing?

PERSONAL REFLECTION PAGE

This is your page to have Breakfast with Jesus. Answer the questions from your heart. Enjoy breaking bread with Jesus. Thank you for sharing a reflection in this book.

Where would you invite Jesus for breakfast?

What would you serve Him?

What would you two talk about?

What does Jesus say that touches your heart?

When He comes again to earth, where would He take you for breakfast?

YOUR PERSONAL RECIPE PAGE

Title of Recipe:

Holy Title you give it:

Submitted by:

Ingredients

...a pinch of "grace
...a dash of "kindness"
...a spoonful of "prayer"
...and a heaping
    Tablespoon of Love

<u>RECIPE FOR A HOLY LIFE</u>

Start with faith and kindness

Mix in gentleness of spirit

Add slowly ...strength and nobility of soul

above the stress and worries in life

Fold in your wonderful personality

Toss with a generous heart smile or two

Pour it in your love mold...God gave you

Yield... one precious blessing to share

at ... BREAKFAST WITH JESUS

EPILOGUE

Just Imagine… as you approach your morning breakfast table… and you see Jesus there waiting for you. Now you have a sacred reminder of the presence of divine love that helps you begin the day nourishing your soul and spirit "in the breaking of the bread". (Luke 24:35)

Perhaps, each day wherever you have breakfast take some quiet time to reflect on Jesus' shared goodness of graces galore in the good times and in times of need and comfort. His very presence is the essence of the meal of love… Eucharist. Let us go forth each day being the "bread of life" for one another.

Sister Ave Clark, O.P.

Every day of the week we can receive the best breakfast meal at the celebration at Mass. A reflection I have to share after receiving the Eucharist is that Jesus is pouring graces of mercy and compassion into our world. I believe his hope for all of us is to get along PEACEFULLY. All of you have your own special relationship and feeling for/with Jesus. Your responses and sharings were extraordinary in this book. I know they touched my heart deeply.

"I am a firm believer that there is no place
where God is not"

(Maya Angelou)

That's my belief also. Viva Jesus Christ.

Joseph (Joe) Clark

ACKNOWLEDGEMENTS

We the authors (brother and sister) would like to acknowledge all the people who shared their favorite breakfast recipe or treat and also with their heart sharing of being in Jesus' presence. That for sure is the best part of this book.

Thank you to Susan Schwemmer... dedicated heart to heart assistant for her encouragement and responding with a gracious "Yes" to write the Prologue for this book. Thank you also to her son, Eric who does a lot of behind the scenes technological help and support.

Thank you to our fine artist, Susan Pussilano, for painting such a "holy" image for this book cover.

Thank you to James Palmaro who shared a special faith poem about Breakfast with Jesus.

Many thanks to Ralph Iskaros who creates a new holy book mark for each book. Ink-It Printers continue to help us with making cards and flyers for our new books and ministry.

Above all... what would we do without our Faith. This book reflects the faith we all share in the "breaking of the bread" and sharing it so that others will recognize Jesus in the countless graces He gives to each one of us for our daily bread.

ABOUT THE AUTHORS

Joseph M. Clark

My name is Joe Clark and I am Sister Ave's younger brother. I am also known as "Jersey Joe" to some family members. Our parents lived in Brooklyn, New York (Paul, Ave and Patty are "Brooklynites") and through eminent domain the city of Brooklyn (took) needed their property and several other neighbors' properties to build a school. So, my family journeyed to the beautiful state of New Jersey and settled in Caldwell where I was born.

The Caldwell property was large with a big house with one bathroom for two adults and four children. Paul was ten years my senior and Ave and Patty were older too! (Don't try to guess their ages...my sisters look very youthful. Boy Joe, are you full of blarney!!!

The years pass swiftly and here we are today. I was a son, brother, husband, father and grandpa and good friend to all. So much went on during those years... it is unbelievable!

Well, Ave asked me to co-author this book with her. I wasn't so keen on the idea since my life is usually a humble, quiet one. I love my faith and the church despite all the challenges of being a good Christian. Then I thought of my faith and I said *Yes* to co-author the book. I have read all your thoughts, sharings, questions and answers and have been deeply touched by all who gave their time and being so real about Jesus' presence in their lives.

I'd like to share about an encounter with Jesus' presence that I received from a young lady who worked in Mountainside Hospital in Glen Ridge, New Jersey. It was during a time I was bringing my mother there for blood transfusions weeks before she passed. In a conversation with that young lady we talked about everything under the sun. We talked about Christ and his giving us a life to live. She asked me, how do you live your life?

I, I, I… didn't know how to answer that, as she was a stranger or... was she Jesus' presence for me. From her desk she gave me a sheet of paper with the title…*What is Life*? (see in book). I have kept that piece of paper, worn by the years' weather, taped on my ice box in the garage since that day. Every day, I see that wonderful saying and read one or more thoughts… it sure has made a difference in my life.

Why do I share this with all of you? After I read your thoughts about Breakfast with Jesus I thought perhaps some of you might like to read it and find its' meaning might just resonate with your heart sharings.

I have wondered over the years about that very kind young lady and I often think of her in prayer… for sharing her faith with me and being Jesus' compassionate presence for me. Perhaps the moments we share with someone extending care and kindness is "Jesus' Manna" from heaven for us.

It truly was a gift to be a co-author of this book…and meet all of you fine people. (No blarney!!)

What is Life?

Life is a challenge............. Meet It
Life is a Gift..................... Accept It
Life is an Adventure........ Dare It
Life is Sorrow.................. Overcome It
Life is a Tragedy.............. Face It
Life is a Duty................... Perform It
Life is a Game................. Play It
Life is a Mystery.............. Unfold It
Life is a Song.................. Sing It
Life is an Opportunity.... Take It
Life is a Journey.............. Complete It
Life is a Promise............. Fulfill It
Life is Beauty.................. Praise It
Life is a Struggle............. Fight It
Life is a Goal................... Achieve It
Life is a Puzzle................ Solve It

If you ever get a chance to go to Denville, New Jersey... stop at Joe's house. He will show you the original worn paper of **What is Life** taped to the ice box in his garage. You can read it together... then have some of his homemade short prayer bread!

Sister Ave Clark, O.P.

Since this is a book about conversations, I decided the authors would share something about who they are and what has touched their life.

An added thought I would like to share is that starting August of 2021 the Dominican Order (which I belong to) is celebrating the 800th Anniversary of the death of St. Dominic... the Holy Founder. The theme for the Jubilee celebration is "At the Table" with St. Dominic which is inspired by the Mascarella table... the table on which the first portrait of St. Dominic was painted shortly after his canonization in 1234 (go online for more information). We Dominicans will celebrate St. Dominic, not as a saint alone on a pedestal, but as a saint enjoying "a table" of fellowship. This Jubilee celebration invites one to reflect on these questions....

What does it mean to be "at table" with St. Dominic here and now?

How does his life and work inspire and encourage us to share our Faith, Hope and Love and our spiritual and material goods so that others may be nourished "at the table"?

How does "the table" become a table for the breaking of the Word and Bread of life?

Hmmmmm, I thought, as I read this and wrote Breakfast with Jesus with my brother Joe. Every day we sit at a table, let us be reminded that to share our faith is a beautiful gift to "break bread" with one another.

Breakfast with Jesus is not about just one table but the many tables Jesus invites us to share a holy presence. Being present with our simplicity, honesty and openness of heart is being Eucharistic people in action. We gather at a table to listen and share and lean on the heart of Jesus' love so we can go out and serve in Jesus' name.

Think of what you share at a table and around a table… not just a meal but your heart to heart conversations sprinkled with a good recipe or 2, 3 or 4 (like in this book), recipes filled with the warmth of loving care. So happy as a Dominican sister I can sit at a table with my brother Joe sharing stories of Breakfast with Jesus.

As many of you know I am an Amityville Dominican sister. I coordinate Heart to Heart Ministry and enjoy sharing retreats and spiritual events. Since the pandemic things have changed and I had to be creative in new ways… zoom retreats, Facebook sunshine chats, a podcast of everyday graces and writing some new books.

When I asked my brother Joe to join me in co-authoring Breakfast with Jesus I crossed my fingers over my heart and prayed he would say *Yes*. At first, he said, "Ahhh I don't know." I said to think about it and added, "Jesus is calling you!" I imagined his Irish smile over the phone. Well as you can see he said Yes!

Whenever our family is together at Joe's home for holidays we gather around the table, hold hands and Joe looks at me to say a grace of thanksgiving… then he adds our dad's favorite grace (in book on memory page). You might just say Jesus is at that table holding hands with all in the family.   Unfortunately, the pandemic has put a temporary halt on these gatherings.

I hope you all enjoyed hearing from the authors. This writing has certainly been a happy adventure about sharing the presence of Jesus' love. May our life like bread "rise up" to greet each new day.

Rise Up ... Like Bread

Rise up...
    like bread
What do you need?
What fulfills you?
What do you hope for?

Rise up ...
    like bread
God's outpouring of daily bread
Remains forever bountiful

Share your recipes of
    Compassion and generosity

Share your friendship of
    Joy and peace graciously

Remember ...
    Do this in memory ...

Rise up ...
    like bread
Share your bread ...
    so others have life
Share your bread ...
    with a stranger ... it is I

Rise up ...
    like bread
    Become the bread that gives life

SPECIAL MENTION

PEOPLE SERVING WITH JESUS' LOVE
(see their sharings inside book)

Barney's Service Station
220-05 Horace Harding Expressway
Bayside, New York 11364
718-428-9600

> Great service with a smile!
> Tony and Vito

Bayside Milk Farm
35-15 Bell Blvd.
Bayside, New York 11361
718-225-0050

> Good food and friendly service!
> Daniel at Deli counter

The "bread" is how we serve and care about each other.
The bread *broken* is how we share and serve one another.

OTHER BOOKS BY SISTER AVE CLARK, O.P.

Lights in the Darkness... for survivors of abuse

Arthur, Thank you for Being Jesus' Love

Heart to Heart Parables: *Sowing Seeds of Peace, Hope, Faith and Love*

A Heart of Courage: *The Ordinary and Extraordinary Becoming Holy*

Be Inspired ... To Love

Books are available on Amazon or by contacting Sr. Ave Clark, O.P. at **Pearlbud7@aol.com** 718-428-2471

BREAKFAST WITH JESUS

... A Holy Invitation with Many Graces

... when they landed, they saw a fire of burning coals there with fish on it, and some bread ... Jesus said to them, "come and have some breakfast."

(John 21:9)

Made in the USA
Middletown, DE
26 September 2021